Milt

The Literary Agenda

Milton's Poetical Thought

MAGGIE KILGOUR

OXFORD
UNIVERSITY PRESS

Great Clarendon Street, Oxford, OX2 6DP,
United Kingdom

Oxford University Press is a department of the University of Oxford.
It furthers the University's objective of excellence in research, scholarship,
and education by publishing worldwide. Oxford is a registered trade mark of
Oxford University Press in the UK and in certain other countries

Published in the United States of America by Oxford University Press
198 Madison Avenue, New York, NY 10016, United States of America

British Library Cataloguing in Publication Data

Data available

Library of Congress Control Number: 2021933675

ISBN 978-0-19-880882-4

Printed and bound by
CPI Group (UK) Ltd, Croydon, CR0 4YY

For my students

Acknowledgements

At Oxford, I owe a great debt to Jacqueline Norton, who knew that I wanted to write this book before I did. Phil Davis, the series editor and my Platonic reader, leapt into the Miltonic conversation with endless enthusiasm. Thanks Phil, for your generosity of spirit, fine ear, and sharp editorial secateurs. Much of the early work was done in the quiet and still air of delightful studies of All Souls College, Oxford, where I enjoyed the good company and cheer especially of Vince Crawford, Silvia Ferrara, Colin Burrow, and Andrew Wynn Owen.

There are three great things about studying Milton. The first is (obviously) Milton. Some authors, even good ones, wear thin after a few years. Not Milton. Age does not wither him; he gets better and more meaningful to me as I grow up. The second thing is the great community of readers of Milton, which goes back to the early editors and includes my constant companions, the best literary critics in our tradition, Dr. Johnson and Samuel Taylor Coleridge. Given the perameters of this series, I cannot even begin to acknowledge properly the many living Miltonists whose writing, talks, and conversations have inspired and informed my understanding of Milton. I feel deeply grateful to be part of such a community.

And the third thing is of course the students who every year discover *Paradise Lost* and open my eyes to new aspects of the text. This book is the product of conversations with the wonderful groups I have been fortunate to work with at McGill over many years. While there have been too many to name you all, I hope you may see yourself in here. In the last few years I have been particularly inspired for this project by working with and being helped by Shaun Ross, Katherine Horgan, Chris Rice, Gabby Samra, Dez Cipollone, Mike D'Itri, Hannah Korell, Tal Golan, Kira Hoelscher, Chloe Holmquist, and, above all, three fine and generous readers: Manuel Cárdenas, Celia Farrow, and (circle wrangler extraordinaire) Leehu Sigler.

As always, my deepest debts are to Brian, passionate reader and writer of poetry, and Cuillin, who howled.

Note to Reader

Unless otherwise noted, all citations of Milton's works are from *The Complete Poetry and Essential Prose of John Milton*, ed. William Kerrigan, John Rumrich, and Stephen M. Fallon (New York: Modern Library, 2007), noted in the text as Kerrigan.

Series Introduction

The Crisis in, the Threat to, the Plight of the Humanities: enter these phrases in Google's search engine and there are 23 million results, in a great fifty-year-long cry of distress, outrage, fear, and melancholy. Grant, even, that every single anxiety and complaint in that catalogue of woe is fully justified—the lack of public support for the arts, the cutbacks in government funding for the humanities, the imminent transformation of a literary and verbal culture by visual/virtual/digital media, the decline of reading ....And still, though it were all true, and just because it might be, there would remain the problem of the response itself. Too often there's recourse to the shrill moan of offended piety or a defeatist withdrawal into professionalism.

The Literary Agenda is a series of short polemical monographs that believes there is a great deal that needs to be said about the state of literary education inside schools and universities and more fundamentally about the importance of literature and of reading in the wider world. The category of 'the literary' has always been contentious. What *is* clear, however, is how increasingly it is dismissed or is unrecognized as a way of thinking or an arena for thought. It is sceptically challenged from within, for example, by the sometimes rival claims of cultural history, contextualized explanation, or media studies. It is shaken from without by even greater pressures: by economic exigency and the severe social attitudes that can follow from it; by technological change that may leave the traditional forms of serious human communication looking merely antiquated. For just these reasons this is the right time for renewal, to start reinvigorated work into the meaning and value of literary reading for the sake of the future.

It is certainly no time to retreat within institutional walls. For all the academic resistance to 'instrumentalism', to governmental measurements of public impact and practical utility, literature exists in and across society. The 'literary' is not pure or specialized or self-confined; it is not restricted to the practitioner in writing or the academic in studying. It exists in the whole range of the world which is its subject-matter: it consists in what non-writers actively receive from writings when, for example, they start to see the world more imaginatively as a result of reading novels and begin to think more carefully about human personality. It comes from literature making available much of human life that would not otherwise be existent to thought or recognizable as knowledge. If it is true that involvement in literature, so far from being a minority aesthetic, represents a significant contribution to the life of human thought, then that idea has to be argued at the public level without succumbing to a hollow rhetoric or bowing to a reductive world-view. Hence the effort of this series to take its place *between* literature and the world. The double-sided commitment to occupying that place and establishing its reality is the only 'agenda' here, without further prescription as to what should then be thought or done within it.

What is at stake is not simply some defensive or apologetic 'justification' in the abstract. The case as to why literature matters in the world not only has to be argued conceptually and strongly tested by thought, it should be given presence, performed and brought to life in the way that literature itself does. That is why this series includes the writers themselves, the novelists and poets, in order to try to close the gap between the thinking of the artists and the thinking of those who read and study them. It is why it also involves other kinds of thinkers—the philosopher, the theologian, the psychologist, the neuro-scientist—examining the role of literature within their own life's work and thought, and the effect of that work, in turn, upon literary thinking. This series admits and encourages personal voices in an unpredictable variety of individual approach and expression, speaking wherever possible across countries and disciplines and temperaments. It aims for something more than intellectual assent: rather the literary sense of what it is like to feel the thought, to embody an idea in a person, to bring it to being in a narrative or in aid of adventurous reflection. If the artists refer to their own works, if other thinkers return to ideas that have marked much of their working life, that is not their vanity nor a failure of originality. It is what the series has asked of them: to speak out of what they know and care about, in whatever language can best serve their most serious thinking, and without the necessity of trying to cover every issue or meet every objection in each volume.

Philip Davis

Contents

Introduction: Milton's Luxurious Imagination

Give me the luxuries of life and I can dispense with the necessities.
Attributed to Oscar Wilde.

There once was a young man of great promise, an oldest son named after his delighted father, who from an early age was astonishingly precocious. He was encouraged and supported by his proud parents, especially his father, a successful and self-made business man, who after a falling out with his own family had had to earn his way in the world. The parents were deeply religious and hoped that their brilliant son might find a good position in the church where he would clearly achieve great things, earning fame for himself while nobly serving God and society. They were certain he would be a man of importance. He had the best tutor and went to an excellent grammar school before heading to Cambridge. But when he finished university, rather than beginning his much anticipated career, he went home and continued to read. Intellectually ambitious and curious, he felt there was still so much he had yet to learn, and he dedicated five more years to studying in order to prepare himself for a great future.

While his parents continued to support this study, the young man increasingly felt the pressure to do something to justify their faith, not to mention financial investment. Some of his friends were beginning to make subtle digs about his putting off his entrance into the 'real world', asking him when he was going to go out and get a job and show the world what he could do. They hinted that he was being unrealistic and selfish, dreaming away the best years of his life when he should be building his future. Though in many ways he was remarkably, even sometimes off-puttingly, self-confident, he himself worried about his tendency to procrastination and his slowness to get out and make his mark. He feared that in taking so long to get ready to do something great he might miss the opportunity to do anything at all. This was complicated further by the fact that as he studied and matured intellectually he felt that the career chosen for him by his well-intentioned parents was not for him. He certainly wanted to do and be something of real significance and spend his life in the most meaningful way possible, but not through preaching. He realized, in fact, that he wanted to be a poet.

The story I am telling here is that of the poet John Milton, but with a few changes (including the welcome one that this might be the story of a young woman), it might be a description of many of my students today who, while not necessarily wanting to become poets themselves, want to spend time studying poetry. Smart, curious, ambitious, they often however do not have the kind of emotional and financial support that Milton had, and find themselves under pressure from their family, friends, and the world around them who expect great things of them. Students of humanities broadly and literature in particular feel vulnerable to accusations that their field is not relevant or useful. They are told that studying such flimsy subjects is selfish, self-indulgent, and elitist (unlike of course the pursuit of altruistic things like Business or Management). They are on a dead-end track that will not lead to a good career; with their abilities, they should do something important with their lives and not swell the sad ranks of aimless and unemployed ex-literature students. Now especially, studying literature seems to many a luxury neither they nor society can afford.

This book is written for these students and others outside universities who feel that reading literature is in itself meaningful and valuable *especially* in a world in which value is measured predominantly in economic terms. It enlists Milton to help them articulate to themselves and to others the importance of reading literary works, especially poetry. Now this might seem an extremely unpromising approach, one that is fatally booby-trapped from the start. To many, Milton seems to embody all the worst things which make the study of literature irrelevant, superfluous to our needs today—a luxury we not only cannot afford but simply do not want anymore. Dead, white, male, a writer of archaic religious poetry that celebrates a God many of us do not believe in and may find repugnant, what good could he be today, even to people who love literature? He is the authoritarian voice of a suspiciously patriarchal past we want to escape. Who would want him on their side?

Clearly I do! And so, in fact, have many revolutionary movements of the last three hundred or so years. While Milton has come to represent in the public imagination (when he figures in it at all) an oppressive patriarchal tradition, in his lifetime and for two centuries after he was a notorious revolutionary, denounced by members of the status quo as a licentious defender of divorce and social upheaval, while celebrated by radical thinkers for his vehement opposition to the tyranny of custom and political oppression. A political maverick and eccentric thinker on matters of religion who believed that each individual had to decide what was right or wrong for himself (and, yes, even sometimes *her*self), he has been deeply inspiring for many later revolutionary movements. Moreover, although the great eighteenth-century literary critic Samuel Johnson famously attacked his 'Turkish contempt of females', many women writers from his own time on have found him a source of inspiration. It is only in the late nineteenth and early twentieth centuries that Milton became a figure for political and poetical orthodoxy, transformed famously also by feminists Sandra Gilbert and Susan Gubar into a looming 'bogey', haunting and stifling female creativity in particular.[1]

In recent years, therefore, there have been a number of fine books written by major scholars to introduce Milton to a wider audience and to defend his value and relevance today.[2] While this book insists passionately that Milton matters now it is not primarily a defence of him. More specifically, it is a defence of the study of literature, especially,

[1] Dr. Johnson, 'Life of Milton', in *Samuel Johnson: Lives of the Poets*, ed. Roger Lonsdale (Oxford: Oxford University Press, 2009), 93. All further citations from Johnson will be from this edition. Sandra Gilbert and Susan Gubar, *The Madwoman in the Attic: The Woman Writer and the Nineteenth-Century Literary Imagination* (New Haven: Yale University Press, 1979). I'll return to Milton and later women writers in my final chapter.

[2] I'd especially recommend John Leonard's *The Value of Milton* (Cambridge: Cambridge University Press, 2016); David Hopkins's *Reading 'Paradise Lost'* (Malden, MA and Oxford: Wiley-Blackwell, 2013); Nigel Smith's *Is Milton Better than Shakespeare?* (Cambridge, MA: Harvard University Press, 2008); and Joseph Wittreich's *Why Milton Matters* (New York: Palgrave Macmillan, 2006). See also my suggestions for further reading at the end of this book.

though not only, poetry, which uses Milton to think through the problems we face today.

Defences of Milton often dwell, understandably, on his advocacy for political freedom and freedom of thought, especially in his most famous political pamphlet, *Areopagitica*, written in 1644 against censorship, in which he cries: 'Give me the liberty to know, to utter, and to argue freely according to conscience, above all liberties' (Kerrigan, 960).[3] In recent years, therefore, Milton may have become better known as a *political* thinker than as a poet. The danger in this is that it puts poetry at the service of politics, replacing an economic standard of measurement with an ideological one. It thus reinforces from the opposite direction the trivialization of the aesthetic, making it subordinate to the message, a means to an end, and so confirms assumptions of systems like the British REF which measure literature by its social impact. It also, I think, does not reflect Milton's own priorities and sense of his real achievement. While Milton devoted almost twenty years of his life to political change, he thought of himself as above all a poet. Even when entering into political debate he is careful to remind his readers that he is a poet, and claims that it is this role that authorizes him to speak on political matters. *Areopagitica* itself is primarily a defence of the power, both social and personal, of reading. It claims that reading promotes independence of thought, and insists that a healthy society would be 'a Nation of readers, and thinkers' who are:

> sitting by their studious lamps, musing, searching, revolving new notions and ideas wherewith to present, as with their homage and their fealty, the approaching reformation; others as fast reading, trying all things, assenting to the force of reason and convincement. What could a man require more from a nation so pliant and so prone to seek after knowledge? What wants there to such a towardly and pregnant soil but wise and

---

[3] While Milton's speech is rousing, his attack on censorship and definition of free speech is limited. He is not what we would call a democrat. For some readers today, this makes him an inadequate role model; see especially Leonard 1–21 for a good account of the issues here. But the rhetorically powerful work has resounded for other writers who have pushed his thinking even further. The fact that *Areopagitica* has inspired thinkers more radical than Milton is evidence that, as I will argue, the value of Milton lies in his excess, the superfluity of meaning that goes beyond his own intentions and control.

faithful laborers to make a knowing people a nation of
prophets, of sages, and of worthies?   (Kerrigan, 957)

In arguing against censorship, moreover, Milton defends the freedom
of the imagination to entertain all possibilities. For him, reading is
how we know the world and encounter both good and evil. It is therefore essential to his exploration of kinds of knowledge in *Paradise Lost*.
Poetry in particular lets us ask and make sense of fundamental questions: Why is there evil in the world? What is freedom, and what
impedes it? Why are men and women unable to make each other
happy? Why do genuine attempts to do good backfire? Are our
individual lives meaningful? Reading Milton as a poet is not to depol-
iticize him, as for Milton religion, sexuality, politics, and poetics,
indeed every aspect of life, are essentially intertwined. The literary is
neither abstracted from life nor a simple expression of history or
political beliefs but the means through which we live and make sense
of our complex lives.

This book thus invokes Milton as a *poetical* thinker: someone who
thinks about and through poetry. It argues that the questions we are
asking today about the place and value of the literary are the ones that
he returns to repeatedly in his works. At the same time, what I believe
makes Milton most useful today is not his likeness to us, but his radical
otherness and strangeness. His very peculiar way of writing, his elaborate and idiosyncratic syntax, dense, compressed images and elaborate similes, his convoluted, circular narrative structure that resists
linear sequence, all these do strange things to our brains. His language
is not as Latinate as some critics have supposed, but he makes the
English language do odd things. Even his spelling makes the familiar
strange; while I'll be citing a modernized edition of Milton's poetry
here, at times I will draw attention to the way in which Milton's original spelling demands us to see deeper meanings in words—to see,
for example, in "L'Allegro" the *holy* day in *holi*day.

Milton's poetic techniques challenge and shake us up, making us
think in unfamiliar ways. In *Paradise Lost* 1, Milton describes Satan's
enormous shield through an epic simile. It is common for epic heroes
to have a big shield; in the ancient world both Achilles and Aeneas
did, and Homer and Virgil describe in detail the decorations engraved
on the surfaces. But Milton is not interested in what is on the shield

but first of all in its impressive size, telling us that it is as big as the moon. But not just any moon; this shield is:

> like the moon, whose orb
> Through optic glass the Tuscan artist views
> At evening from the top of Fesole,
> Or in Valdarno, to descry new lands,
> Rivers or mountains in her spotty globe.   (1.287–91)

Milton here draws attention away from the object itself to a particular act of seeing and a specific seer: Galileo, whom Milton claimed to have met when he was in Italy. At that time the astronomer was old, blind, and under house arrest by the Catholic church for his revolutionary claim that the sun moved around the earth. For the older, blind Milton, the Italian visionary thinker who helped change and indeed reverse our perception of reality offers a model for himself and his poem. *Paradise Lost* is itself a kind of telescope that lets us see the world from a completely new perspective. At times, it too turns our world inside out, asking us to imagine a world completely different from our own, one that is supposed to be better than anything we have known. It expands our imagination and our sense of the possibilities in our lives.

Still, this too may seem rather paradoxical. If Milton shapes our thought through his poetry, how then can he offer us freedom? It sounds like he's trying to make us think like Milton, not think for ourselves. Certainly, in his prose when he is passionately calling for social, religious, and/or political change, Milton is not shy about telling us what he believes and arguing for it vehemently. His tendency there to portray anyone who disagrees with him as a dunce can make him rather unattractive even when he is espousing ideas with which we agree wholeheartedly. So in one of his prose pamphlets, a positive assertion of human freedom of will makes us feel unpleasantly *un*free: 'No man who knows aught can be so stupid to deny that all men naturally were born free, being the image and resemblance of God himself' (*The Tenure of Kings and Magistrates*, 1649; Kerrigan, 1028). Milton not only tells us what he thinks, but insists we think like him or be an idiot.[4]

---

[4] I draw here on John Creaser's contrast between Milton's polemical and poetic voices: '"Fear of change": Closed Minds and Open Forms in Milton', *Milton Quarterly* 42, no. 3 (2008): 161–82.

The poetry works differently, however. On one level of course Milton is using the resources of poetry to guide the reader to think in the specific way he does and to follow in his footsteps. Pushing this to its logical conclusion, Stanley Fish's influential 1967 study, *Surprised by Sin*, argued that the poem restricts its readers' experiences, making us each go through our own individual 'fall', by leading us into interpretive errors and then correcting us. Most notably, Fish claimed, we begin by admiring Satan, but, through the guiding intervention of the narrator, are shown our mistake and returned to the straight and narrow path.

Such a reading is in many ways attractive; it offers coherence and structure, giving us a single pattern that unites a long and complex narrative. It seems rather flattering too, as the poem becomes quite literally *our* story. As I will show later, it is indeed a story about our experience of the world. But like the Milton of the prose, Fish assumes there is one correct and universal view and if you don't see it you are clearly a bit of a blockhead (or worse), as '[t]here is...only one true interpretation of *Paradise Lost*'.[5] But not all readers read alike; many good readers have had very different experiences and interpretations of the poem that feel equally 'true'. As Milton himself noted in *Areopagitica*, our interpretations depend on who we are: 'Wholesome meats to a vitiated stomach differ little or nothing from unwholesome, and best books to a naughty mind are not unappliable to occasions of evil. Bad meats will scarce breed good nourishment in the healthiest concoction, but herein the difference is of bad books, that they to a discreet and judicious reader serve in many respects to discover, to confute, to forewarn, and to illustrate' (Kerrigan, 937–8). Romantics like Blake and Shelley felt deeply that Milton was of the devil's party and were never converted to an alternative; while we may think their reading 'wrong', they opened themselves to the real power of Satan's character.[6] Other readers, in contrast, see the name 'Satan' and decide from the very start that the character is evil. Hardening themselves to Satan's charms, they never need to be converted. My point, to which

---

[5] Stanley Fish, *Surprised by Sin: The Reader in 'Paradise Lost'* (London: Palgrave, 1967), 272.

[6] Blake and Shelley's interpretations of Satan are conveniently collected, along with comments by other Romantics, in Joseph Wittreich, Jr., ed., *The Romantics on Milton: Formal Essays and Critical Asides* (Cleveland and London: The Press of Case Western Reserve University, 1970).

I will return, is that the poem stimulates the reader's experience, but it cannot circumscribe or control it. Poetry is excessive, beyond the author's full control. It is not a dogma, statement, or even a single system but, like Milton's Eden, a place of abundance and growth, alive with possibilities, bursting out in different directions. And this is exactly what makes it so valuable today.

Far from being a control freak choreographing our every move, Milton makes himself surprisingly and indeed movingly vulnerable in his poem, handing to us his fantasies, while not foreknowing or predetermining what we will do with them. He allows us to have free will. That is not to make the text an interpretive free-for-all, however; for Milton, liberty involves responsibility and an awareness of boundaries as constitutive rather than restrictive of freedom. As we'll see, while Adam and Eve live freely in Eden it is a freedom that is 'within bounds' (7.120). The dynamic between author and reader that he creates *through* the poem reflects other patterns of relationship *in* the poem itself—that between teacher and student, husband and wife, God and man—which I will discuss further. These relations are paradoxically both hierarchical and yet complementary forms of exchange and conversation.

This claim may seem to contradict some other common myths about Milton. The narrator of *Paradise Lost* is blind, as Milton himself was at this point, and presents himself as an isolated figure cut off from the world around him by his lack of vision:

> Thus with the year
> Seasons return, but not to me returns
> Day, or the sweet approach of ev'n or morn,
> Or sight of vernal bloom, or summer's rose,
> Or flocks, or herds, or human face divine;
> But cloud instead, and ever-during dark
> Surrounds me, from the cheerful ways of men
> Cut off, and for the book of knowledge fair
> Presented with a universal blank
> Of Nature's works to me expunged and razed,
> And wisdom at one entrance quite shut out.   (3.40–50)

The sense of loss here, of longing to see the beauties of the natural world and the touching 'human face divine', is moving. Yet the narrator turns this isolation into an assertion of an almost stoic autonomy, insisting that:

> More safe I sing with mortal voice, unchanged
> To hoarse or mute, though fall'n on evil days,
> On evil days though fall'n, and evil tongues;
> In darkness, and with dangers compassed round,
> And solitude.   (7.24–8)

This kind of assertion of consistency and integrity in the face of evil has led readers to imagine Milton as a lone genius, set apart from others by both his physical blindness and his imaginative insight. In *Paradise Lost* also he celebrates heroic individuals who alone stand up bravely against a corrupt mob: the angel Abdiel in Books 5–6; Noah and Moses in 11–12, and ultimately their antitype, the Son, who alone in Book 3 volunteers to redeem humankind. Milton himself was such an individual, especially at the Restoration when he continued to argue courageously against the monarchy, knowing he might well be executed for such writings. He knows better than most of us can imagine the true meaning, value, and risks of independent thought. But he also sees its destructive side. Satan also claims heroically that he:

> brings
> A mind not to be changed by place or time.
> The mind is its own place, and in itself
> Can make a Heav'n of Hell, a Hell of Heav'n.
> What matter where, if I be still the same.   (1.252–6)

But this means that he is trapped in Hell even when in Paradise, where:

> within him Hell
> He brings, and round about him, nor from Hell
> One step no more than from himself can fly
> By change of place.   (4.20–3)

In contrast, while the narrator proclaims his own solitary steadfastness, he immediately qualifies his isolation, adding that he is really 'not alone' (7.28) as he is always accompanied by his Muse. In his self-representation, Milton embodies the tension between isolation and togetherness that is at the centre of human existence. Like Satan, we are trapped in our own points of view; like Milton's narrator, we can reach out to others who offer us new ways of seeing. Most of all, perhaps, we are like Adam and Eve at the very end of the poem, wandering through the world solitary, yet hand in hand.

As I suggested earlier, in today's world Milton himself may seem a superfluity, someone who has been made redundant by the march of progress of all kinds. For Milton, in fact, poetry is a necessity precisely because it is superfluous, something fluid that challenges strict boundaries, including those that define and confine us as independent subjects. As many of us have appreciated during the long months of isolation with Covid, literature can make us less lonely, connecting us with others across time and space.

Yet to imagine Milton, a man known for his temperance and moderation, as a Wildean advocate for and even representative of excess or luxury of any kind seems itself somewhat outrageous. Milton is often imagined as severe and puritanical.[7] Certainly he is unlike many of his courtly contemporaries who celebrated unrestrained abandon to sensual pleasures. The fact that Adam and Eve work in his paradise seems evidence of his 'Protestant work ethic'. As we will see more in Chapter 2, work is important for Milton as essential to human creativity and thus dignity. He imagines writing itself as a difficult task, and wants to make his readers also work hard, not to punish them but to exercise and expand their imaginations. Yet Milton is also one of the great celebrators of pleasure and the sensual world. The Hebrew word Eden itself means pleasure, and, as Adam reminds Eve, God 'not to irksome toil, but to delight / ... made us, and delight to reason joined" (9.242–3). In *Paradise Lost*, Milton insists that the true purpose of human life is pleasure, though not mindless or passive pleasure but a creative act that is, as Adam notes, 'to reason joined' (9.243). His vision of prelapsarian happiness as both sensual and rational is politically as well as religiously charged, as he positions himself between the extremes of puritanical denigration of the flesh and libertine abandon to mindless sensuality. It has implications for us today, living at a time when increased utilitarianism makes many think poetry is both too much hard work and a sheer luxury, a time too in which people often seek refuge from excessive work and global uncertainty in more careless and less demanding pleasures.

[7] One famous example of this is Robert Graves's fictionalized version of Milton's first marriage, told from the point of view of Milton's wife, Mary Powell. The caricatured Milton comes off as a pompous sniggering prude; see *Wife to Mr Milton: The Story of Marie Powell* (New York: Noonday Press, 1944).

In a lovely sonnet that he published near the end of his life, Milton argues also for the need to temper the drive to work with a need for pleasure. In it, he asks a friend when they might next get together:

> Lawrence of virtuous father virtuous son,
> Now that the fields are dank, and ways are mire,
> Where shall we sometimes meet, and by the fire
> Help waste a sullen day, what may be won
> From the hard season gaining? Time will run
> On smoother, till Favonius re-inspire
> The frozen earth, and clothe in fresh attire
> The lily and rose, that neither sowed nor spun.
> What neat repast shall feast us, light and choice,
> Of Attic taste, with wine, whence we may rise
> To hear the lute well touched, or artful voice
> Warble immortal notes and Tuscan air?
> He who of those delights can judge, and spare
> To interpose them oft, is not unwise.   ('Sonnet 20')

Milton looks forward to the winter evening they will spend together and its pleasures. We might call this a philosophical poem that expresses a vision of the good life. It shares some elements of other poems of the time which, evoking the classical ideal of 'carpe diem', or seizing the day, recommend retreating from the cares of the world in friendship and wine. But it offers a somewhat different image of pleasure. Central to Milton's idea of a meaningful human existence is friendship. Like most of Milton's sonnets, this is addressed to a particular individual, whose name is given prominence, identifying him as a discrete and specific character, someone whom Milton knew and liked, not just an abstract type. At the same time, the individual is identified as a friend and a member of a family, here tellingly, as a son (a role crucial for Milton, as we will see). While Milton places a great deal of emphasis on the freedoms and responsibilities of the individual to determine his or her own life, the individual is not absolutely autonomous but fully realized only through relations with others. As the poem asks us to see the individual as both distinct and part of a larger whole, it presents time as both specific ('the hard season' of winter, 5) and subsumed into larger rhythms of nature. This means also that while the poem is set in the sullen days of winter, it looks forward to the spring and the new flowering of 'The lily and rose, that neither sowed nor spun' (8). Winter is not an end, it is only a beginning, just as the father himself continues in his son.

The flowers named here are at once natural and symbolic. The lily recalls Christ's advice in Matthew 6:28: 'Consider the lilies of the field, how they grow; they toil not, neither do they spin.' Like many of Christ's parables in the Gospels the phrase is revolutionary in terms of its inversion of expected categories and norms; it calls into question conventional assumptions about values, asking us to think about how we live our lives and spend our time. Christ himself seems to overthrow any incipient work ethic, telling us to live not as workers but as flowers, creatures of nature which do nothing except be beautiful, an idea that Milton emphasizes by adding an extra, luxurious flower: the rose, associated with desire. The poem also argues against the traditional opposition between productive work and idle leisure. The time that first appears to be wasted in sitting by the fire is in fact won (4); the alliteration further binds the two words together. 'Sonnet 20' notes how 'time' runs quickly especially as Milton ages (5). But the poet also makes it move slowly by means of choices of metre and form that measure time carefully. The restrictive and repetitive rhyme scheme of the Petrarchan sonnet, ABBA ABBA CDC EED, creates loops of sound that turn back on themselves and enables Milton to slow the rush of time even as the frequent enjambment of lines makes it move forward. Temporality and temperance are thus linked as ways of arranging and controlling power. The repetition of 'virtuous' in line 1 both suggests an identity between father and son, past and present, and makes the poem feel as if it is not going anywhere in a hurry, curbing the desire to simply 'get ahead'.

The language and thought demand that we spend time to unpack Milton's meaning. Milton makes us slow down. He does not say things directly and quickly. The last two lines especially pull us up through typically Miltonic techniques that demand careful attention. As we will see more later, Milton often gravitates to words that point us in two directions. Here, the word 'spare' reverses meaning as we move from line 13–14: 'He who of those delights can judge, and *spare* / To interpose them oft, is not unwise.' While line 13 tempts us to think that we should 'spare', i.e. refrain *from*, 'those delights', in line 14 we learn that we are actually meant to spare time *for* them. A similar simultaneous offering of antitheses appears in line 14, which shows

Milton's fondness for double negatives. To say that something is 'not unwise' has a very different effect from saying simply that it is 'wise,' even if the expressions seem to mean roughly the same thing. While the meaning of 'wise' is immediately clear, in understanding 'not unwise' we only reach the positive assertion after a complex mental process that demands us to think of something negative (unwise) and also to negate that negative (not). The couplet contains a process of discrimination that unfolds over time: we must think about both sparing (giving up) pleasure and sparing (making) time for pleasure, and also about being wise and unwise at the same time. The poem advocates and demonstrates a form of wisdom that comes from a recognition of the value and, equally essential, the pleasure of taking time and thinking things through slowly, acknowledging all possibilities and making careful choices.

As in many other of his sonnets, Milton presents himself as speaking directly to a friend. Although the friend does not reply, the poem suggests the opening up of dialogue, a conversation to be continued by the fire, with a glass of wine, a 'neat repast', and accompanied by music. For Milton, conversation is the essence of friendship and, especially, marriage. He famously argued that 'a meet and happy conversation is the chiefest and the noblest end of marriage' (*Doctrine and Discipline of Divorce*, 1644; Kerrigan, 871) and in *Paradise Lost*, Adam asks God for a helpmeet who will 'solace his defects' through 'conversation' (8.418–19). Milton's ideal world, the embodiment of the good life, is of course the garden of Eden, which he imagines as a place of constant talk. His poetry is full of dialogues and debates which are intended to generate further discussions with the reader. 'Sonnet 20' does not speak explicitly about poetry of course. But the simple fact that it is a poem is itself essential, suggesting how it is through the form of poetry, with its flexibility, its ability to hold and consider contrary things together ('not unwise'), its sheer aesthetic beauty in excess of basic human needs, that we may glimpse the good life. Wilde was right: it is the luxuries that define us, especially the essential luxury of art. While the flowers in 'Sonnet 20' look back to the Gospel episode, flowers are also a traditional image for poetry itself. English writers in particular love to pun on the correspondence between poesy and posies. For Milton, poetry offers us a chance to slow down, look carefully at the world around us, and reflect on our lives.

For Wilde, what makes us humans are not the bare necessities needed to sustain life, such as food and sex, natural needs which we share with other animals, but the superfluous things that make our life meaningful, above all art and especially the verbal art in which he excelled. A similar idea is central to Shakespeare's *King Lear* in which the king, stripped down to nothing by his abdication of all the supposedly superficial things that he discovers too late made him *King* Lear, recognizes the poverty of the concept of mere need:

> O, reason not the need! Our basest beggars
> Are in the poorest thing superfluous.
> Allow not nature more than nature needs,
> Man's life is cheap as beast's.   (*King Lear* 2.4.264–7)[8]

Like Shakespeare and Wilde, Milton defends what is traditionally seen as superfluous against something else that is defined as necessary and important. The ideal world of Eden is a place of excess and exuberance; it oozes life with its 'umbrageous grots and caves / Of cool recess, o'er which the mantling vine / Lays forth her purple grape, and gently creeps / Luxuriant' (4.257–60). Admiring Milton's vast universe, the eighteenth-century critic Joseph Addison marveled at the 'Wantonness of a luxurious Imagination'.[9]

Milton's language—especially, in the description above, that amazingly sensuous word *umbrageous* which is so delicious to say out loud—shows a delight in luxuriance, as Milton wantons in a world in which everything is overflowing and intertwined. His Paradise is no Puritan or Platonic abstraction; it has 'Groves whose rich trees wept odorous gums and balm' (4.248) and rivers that 'With mazy error under pendant shades / Ran nectar ... / Poured forth profuse on hill and dale and plain' (4.239–40, 243). Milton particularly wants us to appreciate just how great it smells, with its 'groves of myrrh, / And flow'ring odors, cassia, nard, and balm' (5.292–3). Such sensuality is very different from the thoughtless bodily abandon celebrated by some royalists of Milton's time. As I will suggest more in Chapter 2, this fertile and profuse Eden

[8] Cited from *The Riverside Shakespeare*, ed. G. Blakemore Evans (Boston: Houghton Mifflin, 1974). All further citations from Shakespeare will be from this edition.

[9] Joseph Addison, *Spectator* 315, 1 March 1712; cited in John Leonard, *Faithful Labourers: A Reception History of 'Paradise Lost', 1667–1970*. 2 vols. Oxford: Oxford University Press, 2013; 1:715.

is a garden of poetry itself, the fountain of all human creativity, including Milton's capacious and excessive epic, a place invented by a creating God who is himself the spirit of the poetic imagination.

Through this book I will trace Milton's thinking about the role of the poet and place of poetry in the world. This inevitably changed over time, from the idealism of a young man, influenced by humanist thinkers like Philip Sidney, to a more disillusioned yet still astonishingly hopeful writer who had witnessed the failure of a revolution in which he had fervently believed. I begin in Chapter 1 with Milton's beginning as a writer. Formally experimental, wide-ranging in subject and genre, Milton's early poems are united by questions concerning what it means to be a poet, what good poetry can do in the world, and how fictions can tell the truth. The second chapter reads *Paradise Lost* as a poem about poetry and what it means to be a creator. Milton's epic both describes the place of poetry in the ideal world of Eden, and, with the figures of the narrator and Satan, suggests its power and dangers in the fallen world. The final chapter looks at Milton's two last published new poems, *Paradise Regained* and *Samson Agonistes*, as works concerned with what it means to be a reader. They look forward to future writers and readers who will continue to ask the questions Milton demands of us: what role do making and reading poetry play in our lives and understanding of ourselves and the world around us? In today's world, with its urgent need for political, economic, and social change, in what sense is making/reading poetry not a frivolous pursuit but a meaningful action? Why do and should we keep reading Milton in particular? Milton insists that poetry enriches the experience of both writers and readers; it makes us creative, and alive, fully realized, human beings. It gives us knowledge of truths we otherwise would never apprehend. That is why I want him on my side, and why I believe that one of the best ways to argue for the importance of literature today is to stop and 'waste a sullen day' ('Sonnet 20', 4), or two, with him, listening carefully to what he has to say.

1

Born to Write

How to Make a Renaissance Poet

In retrospect, of course, Milton may seem born ready to write *Paradise Lost*. Much of his early poetry looks like a trial run for the great epic, and it is exciting to trace the way the later verse is foreshadowed in the earlier. But Milton himself did not have the luxury of hindsight or know as clearly as we do where he was heading. His involvement in the political and social turmoil during the 1640s meant that when he first appeared in print it was as a writer on politics and divorce. His first collection of verse was not published till January 1646 (though dated 1645) when he was 38 years old, and *Paradise Lost* did not appear till over twenty years later, in 1667.

Such delay itself was not easy for an ambitious young man like Milton. Encouraged by his loving parents, he hoped to do and be something great. Looking back in 1642, he noted how his teachers, parents, and he himself believed from early on that 'by labor and intent study (which I take to be my portion in this life) joined with the strong propensity of nature, I might perhaps leave something so written to aftertimes, as they should not willingly let it die' (*The Reason of Church Government*, 1642; Kerrigan, 840). At the same time, however, he felt equally that he should not rush hastily into a career and needed to take time to prepare himself for his future. So he wrote in a letter to his best friend Charles Diodati in 1637: 'You ask what I am thinking of? So help me God, an immortality of fame. What am I doing? Growing my wings and practicing flight. But my Pegasus still raises himself on very tender wings. Let me be wise on my humble level' (Kerrigan, 775). At times, his aspiration to soar to great achievements and make his mark in the world seems so intense he has difficulty restraining himself. He was acutely self-conscious about what he described as 'my tardy moving' and 'a certain belatedness', which made it appear to others as if he were escaping into a dream world and wasting his time and talents ('Letter to a Friend', *c.*1633; Kerrigan, 770–1). The early poems show a young man who, like many thoughtful people today, had grand dreams of future greatness but was not yet certain of who or what he would be, and who needed time to choose the most meaningful way to spend his life.

Given Milton's abilities and the expectations of the time, moreover, it seemed that he was destined for a career in the Church. Although John Milton Sr. was a successful businessman, he never seems to have pressured or even expected his brilliant son to follow in his footsteps, but hoped he might pursue a calling which would enable him to nobly serve God and his country. Milton's education at one of London's finest schools and later at Cambridge would have prepared him well for the clergy, a career that ideally would have brought worldly fame and status as well as spiritual satisfaction.

It is interesting, if sometimes scary, to think about how education shapes the ways people think, a matter that Milton, later a teacher, did consider very seriously. In 1644 he published a tract *Of Education*, in which he loftily asserted that: 'The end then of learning is to repair the ruins of our first parents by regaining to know God aright, and out of that knowledge to love him, to imitate him, to be like him as we may the nearest by possessing our souls of true virtue, which, being united to the heavenly grace of faith, makes up the highest perfection' (Kerrigan, 971). He believed that education serves a spiritual function: as we'll see further in the next chapter, knowledge, often thought of as evil because of the biblical story of the fall of Adam and Eve, is redemptive when used properly. At the same time, Milton adhered to a general humanist belief that education should have a practical role in this world, producing 'renowned and matchless men' who would be able to use their knowledge for the benefit of his society: 'I call therefore a complete and generous education that which fits a man to perform justly, skillfully, and magnanimously all the offices both private and public of peace and war' (Kerrigan, 973–4).

Although Milton was highly critical of the education system that had produced him, the system was also intended to create good, wise, and capable men who could take a leading role in the church or government. For this purpose, schoolboys were taught to speak well and to organize ideas effectively to persuade their audience. Students were commonly required to display their wit and skill by debate. They would be asked to prepare both sides of an argument and not told which side they would present until the last minute. This kind of assignment encourages the organization of ideas into black and white, pro and con, categories. At university, Milton delivered some speeches of this kind, which he thought skilful or at least interesting enough to publish at the end of his life. The first of these *Prolusions*, 'Whether Day or Night is the More Excellent', is a good example of the kind of trivial topic often assigned and the starkly dualistic argument it fosters. Milton insists that day is good, the realm of light, clarity, and all positive things, while night is bad, the realm of darkness, and the time when wicked spirits come out. To insist that one time of day is somehow morally superior than the other seems silly; the exercise is clearly purely rhetorical and obviously does not reflect anything that Milton might have believed at this time. Debates are training for decision-making, as they allow us to weigh two opinions and choose one as true, but the point of these particular exercises was not to find 'the truth' but to win the argument, and Milton would have been fully prepared to make the counterargument with equal vehemence. Such schooling prepared him well for his later career as a political polemicist.

But this method of argumentation was also liberating, allowing Milton to indulge his imagination freely, unhampered by questions of truth, belief, or sincerity. At the same time as fostering reductively oppositional and competitive thinking, such exercises opened up a space of creative freedom that could encourage students to entertain two contradictory points of view at the same time. This imaginative expansion was reinforced by other common school exercises that allowed students to see the world from different points of view. As well as debating different positions, students were asked to make speeches in the voice of characters, historical and mythological, putting themselves in situations alien to their own. Students learned Latin and Greek by translating and then imitating classical authors, seeking to master the verbal skills and techniques of ancient poets and to transform them into English (and often then back into Latin). Today we tend to think of imitation as a deadening practice that stifles authentic creativity, the opposite of what we call 'originality'. But at its best, encountering the minds of others through translation and adaptation could (and can!) be exhilarating. It taught students to think as an other, through alien words if not literally eyes. The goal of such learning was to produce not slavish imitators but inventive writers who had absorbed classical techniques and made them their own. Students tried on the voices of others in order to develop their own. Going out of oneself and thinking like someone else was ultimately a step toward learning to think for oneself, as knowledge of others leads to self-knowledge.

Debating, public speaking, reading and writing poetry were central to the training offered by the best schools like Milton's. It may seem strange to us, but again the goal of such education was at heart utilitarian, intended to produce informed and active citizens. Students learned what we now call (often with a grimace) 'transferable skills' that could be applied to important public careers. Using language effectively was seen as particularly essential for future preachers, who would deliver resounding sermons, and for would-be lawyers, who would argue cases and jostle for positions of power. Writing poetry could be a method of self-promotion and display. A similar logic drives current claims that the acquisition of skills of analysis and communication through the study of English prepares students for other kinds of jobs.

My experience as both a student and teacher has taught me, however, that there is, fortunately, always a big gap between what teachers think they are teaching and what students actually learn. Like poetry, education is essentially excessive, containing the potential to do more than and even the opposite of its original purpose. It depends so much on the individual students. It is hard not to think that this kind of training had an unintended, less practical, yet ultimately truly revolutionary, effect, stimulating imaginations and so spurring the astonishing creative boom in England in the late sixteenth century, with great poets like Sidney, Spenser, Jonson, Donne, and, above all, Shakespeare. In particular, making speeches from the point of view of different characters must have had an impact on some of the schoolboys who were unable to secure positions as lawyers or clergymen, and who therefore stumbled into a new profession that was opening up: that of playwright.[1]

---

[1] The job market changed rapidly in the late sixteenth century in ways reminiscent of the post-WWII west. In England, the Reformation created new administrative positions

A good number of Milton's early poems probably began life as school exercises. Some are structured like debates, like the Latin poem 'That Nature does not suffer from old age', which takes a stance in a heated contemporary controversy over whether the natural world decays or not. Other poems of greater complexity and interest adapt the debate more subtly as a means for Milton to think through his own future and the kind of poet he might be, as in the case of 'L'Allegro' and 'Il Penseroso', and *A Mask*. I will return to the last of these in particular a bit later.

As a student, Milton would also have been expected to compose funeral elegies on the death of public figures. Such deaths were pounced upon as opportunities to master literary conventions, refine verbal skills, and gain a reputation. Milton, however, has sometimes been seen as particularly ghoulish for the remarkable number of such elegies he produced as a young man. A striking cluster of these were written around the time he was 17, a period which seems to have had a high mortality rate. Milton composed Latin poems on the deaths of two university officials, the Cambridge Beadle and Vice Chancellor, and on those of two ecclesiastical authorities, the Bishops of Winchester and of Ely, and, in what he claimed was his first poem written in English, 'On the Death of a Fair Infant Dying of a Cough', on that of one baby.

Funeral elegies generally have a fairly formulaic structure: they begin with lamentation, usually complain of the bitterness and injustice of death, then ultimately turn towards a final consolation through the discovery that the dead live on through a power greater than death. In classical poetry, eternal life is guaranteed through poetry itself which immortalizes the subject (as the poem itself proves); in Christian writing, it is offered through the promise of a spiritual afterlife. The language, sentiment, and structure of Milton's early poems adhere to these expected conventions. The speaker rails against death's undiscriminating power and its cruel mockery of human aspirations, and complains that the dead did not deserve to die. But in

which in turn required an expanded education system to prepare qualified workers. But by the end of the century there were fewer jobs even as there were more graduates; overeducated and underemployed students fluent in writing and arguing, with highly developed imaginations, had to find other kinds of work. Fortunately, the newly created theatres offered new possibilities of employment.

the end, lamentation turns to celebration: 'On the Death of the Bishop of Ely' ends with the Bishop's apotheosis, in which he leaves 'the foul prison' of the earth for the 'stars on high' (46, 48), and 'Elegy 3', with a dream vision of the dead Bishop of Winchester welcomed joyously into a celestial paradise.

In general, tied to school assignments and conventional occasions, Milton's early verse should not be read as expressing his sincere opinions or feelings any more than we should think that he really thought day better than night. Most of these early elegies were written about people he did not know or care about. At 17 especially, Milton is himself mostly untouched by death; death was not entirely real, simply a pretext for poetic fictions and exercises. Yet the young Milton has a remarkable ability to seize potentially superficial exercises and dig out their deeper meaning. They offer him opportunities for creativity and discovery, opening up a space for him within tradition. They allow him to see what the poetic tradition offers him—and vice versa.

It may be in fact that Milton was attracted to the elegy genre because it allowed him to address concerns he had already formulated; equally possibly, the acts of writing this cluster of elegies in this year of many deaths made the 17-year-old start thinking more seriously about his own future (or indeed possible lack thereof). Because of their subject, elegies made him confront death and loss, subjects that later would grip him deeply. Most importantly, they also seem to have made him start thinking seriously about poetry itself, what it does, and why he might write it, beyond showing everyone how clever he was as he prepared to be something else. Writing poetry might itself be the best way in which he could do something important and meaningful in the world.

Renaissance Debates on Poetry

But what did it mean to be a poet in Milton's time? What was poetry thought to do, and why would a grown man who wanted to contribute to his society spend his life writing it?

For a man of Milton's class, poetry at this time was both central and peripheral, everywhere and nowhere. As I have suggested, it was an important part of education. But as I have also noted, reading and writing poetry was seen as merely a means to an end, not an end in itself. Being a poet was certainly not a full-time job but something that you did as a supplement to *real* work in law, government, or the ministry, domains in which you made your mark. Poetry was generally viewed as the ornament of a gentleman, a hobby, and not a career by which a writer might support himself. Once again, poetry appears a luxury, something decorative and delightful but superfluous, peripheral to real economic and political power.

For many of Milton's time, moreover, poetry's excess was a sign of something more sinister. Current attacks on the humanities are themselves part of a venerable tradition of distrusting art generally. According to Plato, all art is a copy of a material world which is itself merely a copy of the ideal forms that are the only reality. Distanced at two degrees from the truth, art is an illusion, the opposite and indeed enemy of what is permanent and enduring. It blocks us from seeing the reality beyond the world of illusion, and leaves us trapped in fantasy, like the inhabitants of Plato's cave who think that shadows are real. Poets, who make up these fictions, are just plain liars. Opposed to reason, the imagination or fancy appears a capricious and potentially anti-social faculty. In the *Republic*, therefore, Plato claimed that poetry creates social unrest, and so poets should be banned from his ideal society.

In sixteenth- to seventeenth-century England, this long-standing Platonic anxiety about images was boosted by the Protestant disapproval of luxury and fear of what was seen as Catholic idolatry. Today, it is feared that the pursuit of poetry leads to a wasted life; for early modern Protestants, it could take you straight to hell. So Stephen Gosson argued that 'verses' were the first step on the slippery slope 'to piping, from piping to playing, from play to pleasure, from pleasure to sloth, from sloth to sleep, from sleep to sin, from sin to death, from death to the Devil'.[2] The imagination was thought to feed and be fed by sexual desire: tellingly, the word 'fancy' can be both a synonym for the imagination and a verb meaning to want or desire. Although

---

[2] Gosson's diatribe appears in the delightfully titled attack on the stage very typical of this kind of writing at this time: *The Schoole of Abuse Containing a Pleasant Invective Against Poets, Pipers, Players, Jesters, and such Like Caterpillers of a Common Wealth; Setting up the Flag of Defiance to their Mischevious Exercise, and Overthrowing their Bulwarks, by Profane Writers, Natural Reason and Common Experience ....by Stephan Gosson Stud. Oxon* (London: By Thomas Dawson for Thomas Woodcocke, 1587), 12 (B3). (I have modernized Gosson's spelling.)

critics like Gosson were suspicious of poetry and rhetoric generally, they focused particular attention on the new medium of theatre which was also seen as an idolatrous art that lured people away from church attendance and so from God. Theatres were known as pick-up joints. Also deeply worrying was the fact that in the theatre people dress up and pretend to be other than who they are. The suspicion that imaginative works generally lead to the confusion of illusion and reality, fiction and truth, is a concern of much literature of Milton's time, appearing perhaps most famously in Cervantes's *Don Quixote* (1605), in which the deluded Don believes he lives in a chivalric romance. In Milton's *A Mask*, the song of Comus's mother, the enchantress Circe, which 'in pleasing slumber lulled the sense, / And in sweet madness robbed it of itself' (260–1), suggests the dangerously sirenic power of a poetry that alienates us from our true selves and reality. Similar worries about the fragile boundary between imagination and reality are still with us, most often in fearful claims that the representation of violence in film and TV leads to violent acts in real life. The belief that art is unreal and deluding in comparison to some other substantial and real entity is echoed also in complaints that literature distracts students from more meaningful and useful subjects. We may retain more of a 'Puritan' outlook than we think. Now, however, the reality to which fictions are contrasted is sadly most often neither God nor a Platonic ideal but simply that most material substance: money.

The origins of this line of thought in Plato, a thinker admired greatly by many Renaissance writers, is obviously unfortunate. It gives the philistine camp formidable authority and weight. Renaissance poets therefore spent a fair amount of energy trying to prove that Plato did not *really* mean what he seems to say in the *Republic*. They noted that he was a poet himself, who wrote fictitious dialogues. Philip Sidney thus asserted that 'truly even Plato whosoever well considereth shall find that in the body of his work, though the inside and strength were philosophy, the skin, as it were, and beauty depended most of poetry',[3] while in his early poem 'Of the Platonic Idea' Milton says Plato is 'the greatest storyteller' (38). It was commonly asserted also that Plato (who had celebrated poetry in another dialogue, the *Ion*)

---

[3] *Sir Philip Sidney: The Major Works*, ed. Katherine Duncan-Jones (Oxford: Oxford University Press, 1989), 213. All further citations will be to this edition.

was only attacking *bad* poets, and writers insisted that *they* of course were not themselves one of those.

Sidney's famous *Defence of Poesy*, which was written around 1579 in response to Gosson's rant, does not just defend poetry; it insists that it is the highest of all the arts and forms of knowledge. While Sidney admits sadly that there are too many writers in his own time who use poetry merely to make money, he insists that its true function is to enlighten us.[4] He reminds readers that there is another ancient tradition of seeing the poet not as liar but as a prophet and seer: in Latin, a *vates*. Even more, Sidney sees the poet, a name which in Greek means 'maker', as a second God whose power remakes the world. While other disciplines are bound by the law of nature, poetry is the realm of freedom:

> Only the poet, disdaining to be tied to any such subjection, lifted up with the vigor of his own invention, doth grow in effect another nature, in making things either better than nature bringeth forth, or, quite anew, forms such as never were in nature, as the Heroes, Demigods, Cyclops, Chimeras, Furies, and such like: so as he goeth hand in hand with nature, not enclosed within the narrow warrant of her gifts, but freely ranging only within the zodiac of his own wit. Nature never set forth the earth in so rich tapestry as divers poets have done; neither with so pleasant rivers, fruitful trees, sweet-smelling flowers, nor whatsoever else may make the too much loved earth more lovely. Her world is brazen, the poets only deliver a golden.   (216)

Unlike the historian and scientist who are bound by the facts, the poet is free to imagine better worlds. Moreover, unlike the philosopher, who also can tell us about better worlds, the poet moves us to try to realize them by stimulating our emotions. Against Plato's concern that poetry misleads, Sidney draws on the famous formula of the classical poet-critic Horace who had said that poetry must be both delightful

---

[4] While we generally think of sixteenth- to seventeenth-century England as a 'Golden Age' of literature that produced Sidney, Shakespeare, Marlowe, Jonson, Donne, and Milton, writers themselves were highly critical and often depict English literature as in a dark age.

(*dulce*) and educative (*utile*).[5] Although delight might again seem something superfluous to basic needs, it is absolutely essential to poetry's power. It is only *because* it delights us that poetry is able to teach us in ways that philosophy cannot. So Sidney claims:

> Now therein of all sciences (I speak still of human, and according to the human conceit) is our poet the monarch. For he doth not only show the way, but giveth so sweet a prospect into the way, as will entice any man to enter into it. Nay, he doth, as if your journey should lie through a fair vineyard, at the first give you a cluster of grapes, that full of that taste, you may long to pass further. He beginneth not with obscure definitions, which must blur the margin with interpretations, and load the memory with doubtfulness; but he cometh to you with words set in delightful proportion, either accompanied with, or prepared for, the well enchanting skill of music; and with a tale forsooth he cometh unto you, with a tale which holdeth children from play, and old men from the chimney corner. And, pretending no more, doth intend the winning of the mind from wickedness to virtue—even as the child is often brought to take most wholesome things by hiding them in such other as have a pleasant taste. (226–7)

I quote this at such length because the vivid scenes that Sidney paints here, with their luscious metaphors and deftly sketched portraits of spell-bound listeners, demonstrate exactly how poetic language grabs and focuses our attention by its detailed particularity. It lets us both see the world around us through new eyes and also imagine how our world might be other than it is.

Milton's Defence of Poetry: 'To His Father'

In many ways Sidney and Gosson represent two extremes in a perennial debate about poetry. Is the poet a god, or a liar? Does poetry reveal or hide the truth? Is it something or nothing?

---

[5] See *Ars poetica*, 343, in Horace, *Satires. Epistles. The Art of Poetry*, trans. H. Rushton Fairclough, Loeb Classical Library (Cambridge, MA: Harvard University Press, 1978).

Milton's Latin poem 'To His Father' recalls these arguments. Probably written in the 1630s as Milton approached his thirtieth birthday, it announces his own explicit 'coming out' as a poet. The tone is defensive as the pretext of the poem (which may or may not of course be true) is that Milton's father, who has spent so much money on his son's expensive education, is now disappointed to hear that his talented heir wants to be a mere poet. Milton uses his training in debate to convince John Milton Sr. that being a poet is of value (an argument useful for English students as well as poets today). This situation of generational conflict between the two John Miltons could easily have become a story of rebellion in which the son rejects the father's materialistic values in defence of a higher, unmaterialistic good. Milton's Protestant father had himself broken with his Catholic family over religion. But, typically, Milton is determined to keep the father-son relation non-adversarial. While he clearly differentiates himself from the father whose name he shares, he insists on the loving continuity between father and son. In *Paradise Lost* Satan resents God's gifts to him as unfairly burdensome. In contrast, here Milton dutifully acknowledges his father's generosity which has in fact enabled him to become a poet. He confesses how difficult it is to repay what he owes his father for his support and love:

> best father, she [the Muse] is devising this song, a slight work, and we ourselves do not know a more suitable offering in payment for your gifts, although the greatest offering could not repay your gifts, still less could arid thanks which is given in vain words be equal to your gifts. But still, this page shows our account, and we have numbered on this paper what wealth we have: of which I have none except what golden Clio [the Muse] has given, which my sleep has spawned in a remote cavern, and the laurel groves in the sacred wood, the shades of Parnassus.
>
> (6–16; Kerrigan, 221)

The father's substantial financial gifts can only be met by the son's 'slight' poetic one (the Latin adjective, '*exiguus*' used here means further 'meagre', 'trifling').

At first this looks like an unfair trade in which the father is being short-changed. But then the poem abruptly turns to insist on the value and power of poetry:

do not look down on the poet's work, divine song; nothing more commends our celestial origins and heavenly seeds, nothing, because of its origin, more commends the human mind, keeping the sacred traces of Promethean fire. The gods love song, song has power to stir the shuddering depths of Tartarus and bind the gods of the deep, and constricts the harsh shades with threefold adamant. With song the priestesses of Phoebus and the trembling, palemouthed Sibyls uncover the secrets of the distant future. (17–25; p. 221)

Contrary to appearances, it is a great thing to be a poet! Poetry lets you conquer hell and death itself. Not everyone is up to this heroic feat, however. Being such a poet demands discipline and restraint; as the idealistic young Milton claims in another tract: 'he who would not be frustrate of his hope to write well hereafter in laudable things ought himself to be a true poem, that is, a composition and pattern of the best and honorablest things—not presuming to sing high praises of heroic men or famous cities, unless he have in himself the experience and the practice of all that which is praiseworthy' (*An Apology for Smectymnuus*, 1642; Kerrigan, 850). For Milton, the poet who aspires to the highest form of poetry, epic, must be chaste. This is not because Milton is prudishly disgusted by the body: as we'll see, in *Paradise Lost* he celebrates Adam and Eve's nudity and carefree sexuality. But it is because erotic and poetic energy are linked that the ambitious young poet wants to channel bodily passion into poetic creativity. To become a truly great poet takes enormous physical as well as intellectual self-control.

The rewards for such self-restraint are great, however. In 'To His Father', Milton draws on Sidney to celebrate poetry as the highest form of knowledge: that of the nature of the universe and the gods themselves. Such knowledge lifts humans to the heavens and makes us immortal. While the poem begins with the son apologizing to his father that he has so little to return for all he has been given, it ends by subtly turning the tables. Although he praises his generous father for giving him everything, he manages to note there is one thing that the father's wealth cannot buy: 'What greater things could a father have bestowed, even if Jove himself had given all (*with the exception of heaven*)?' (95–6, pp. 223–4; emphasis added). But heaven is the only thing worth getting, and the son alone can get it, both for himself and for his father, through writing poetry. The poem thus asserts the son's higher power, though crucially without setting it antagonistically against that of his father. The father's ephemeral financial gift has been accepted and transformed into the son's eternizing poetic gift. Through poetry Milton pays tribute to and so immortalizes his father; poetry, not material wealth, is what is truly substantial and lasting.

First Beginnings: 'On the Morning of Christ's Nativity. Composed 1629'

> Christ's place indeed is with the poets. His whole conception of Humanity sprang right out of the imagination and can only be realised by it.
>
> Oscar Wilde, *De Profundis*[6]

Milton's defence of poetry in 'To His Father' is fleshed out throughout his first collection of writings, the 1645 *Poems*. The volume is divided into two parts, with a series of poems written mostly in English followed by a second group mostly in Latin, the language in which much poetry was still written. Made up of poems written not only in different languages but also in different genres—elegies, sonnets, debates, translations of biblical psalms, even drama—and on a wide range of subjects spanning birth to death, the collection shows off Milton's skill and mastery of traditional forms, and announces him to the world as an important new poet. The whole is arranged to tell his version of how, and why, he became a poet. It makes clear what kind of writer Milton thinks he is, and what he believes poetry can and should do.

The volume and story begins with 'On the Morning of Christ's Nativity. Composed 1629.' While not Milton's earliest poem in terms of actual chronology, it is an appropriate start to the collection, a poetic manifesto that offers the reader a guide for the other works to follow. The inclusion of the date is significant: it makes Milton's poetic career seem to begin in 1629, the year in which he turned 21. The title puns on the word 'on', drawing on its double sense to suggest it is not

---

[6] Cited from the *Complete Works of Oscar Wilde*, with an introduction by Vyvyan Holland, reprint (London and Glasgow: Collins, 1971), 923.

only written *about* Christ's birthday but also *on* the very day itself. The poem thus announces simultaneously Christ's birth and Milton's birth as poet (conveniently, Milton was also a December baby, born on 9 December 1608). It connects these two events, as Milton sees his poetry as inspired by the birth of Christ. While Sidney had imagined the poet as a god, Milton imagines God as a poet. For him, creativity is the essence of the divine, and in *Paradise Lost* God will be celebrated as the 'Maker omnipotent' (4.725) and 'The great Creator' (7.567). More specifically, like other Christians of the time, as well as Oscar Wilde much later, Milton sees Christ, the Son of God, as the embodiment of divine creative energy, and thus the source and model for all human creativity, especially Milton's own.

My concern in this book is not of course with Milton as a religious thinker but Milton as a poetical thinker. But for him the two realms are intertwined as his creativity is stimulated by his Christian belief. I am also aware, however, that Milton's conspicuous Christianity may seem inherently off-putting or at least alienating to many readers today. A lack of knowledge of the Christian tradition may seem to disadvantage the modern reader, and certainly non-Christians may not grasp immediately how radically unorthodox and idiosyncratic Milton's religious thought is. Yet in some ways such readers may be better able to see the significance of Milton's religious beliefs for his poetics, and to grasp how and why in history Christianity has been so inspiring for poetry in general.

As often noted, the Bible is itself great literature, and today is frequently taught simply as such. But it also inspired an enormous amount of great art of all kinds. For poets especially, it is thrilling that the Bible begins with God's creation of the world through speech. In Genesis, God speaks the world into being: 'God said, Let there be light: and there was light' (Genesis 1:3). His creative power is verbal, identified with the concept of the Word: 'In the beginning was the Word, and the Word was with God, and the Word was God. The same was in the beginning with God. All things were made by him; and without him was not any thing made that was made' (John 1:1–3). As Sidney had argued, the poet is indeed like God, as his verbal art copies God's originating act. According to the Ten Commandments also, God cannot be represented in 'graven images', but reveals himself to us through language, both in the Bible itself, traditionally believed to be 'God's word', and also in specific incidents in which he speaks to select figures such as the prophet Moses. The Old Testament God is quite talkative; in the New Testament, Christ is a skilled story-teller who teaches through parables.

In Christianity, the historical figure of Jesus Christ is not only the Son of God, but he is imagined specifically as the Word of God made flesh: 'And the Word was made flesh, and dwelt among us, (and we beheld his glory, the glory as of the only begotten of the Father,) full of grace and truth' (John 1:14). Milton's subject in this poem is this moment of incarnation when the divine creative power comes to earth in the newborn baby and also in Milton's own poem.

But the poem seems to approach its subject obliquely, circling around it from a distance. Even a reader unfamiliar with Christian doctrine might note that, despite the title, there is oddly little descrip-tion of an actual nativity scene in this poem.[7] The baby in the manger appears briefly, but is quickly displaced by a series of elaborate poetic images and scenes which describe the world around him and how it is affected by his coming:

> It was the winter wild,
> While the Heav'n-born-child,
>   All meanly wrapped in the rude manger lies;
> Nature in awe to him
> Had doffed her gaudy trim
>   With her great master so to sympathize:
> It was no season then for her
> To wanton with the sun her lusty paramour.
>
> Only with speeches fair
> She woos the gentle air
>   To hide her guilty front with innocent snow,
> And on her naked shame,
> Pollute with sinful blame,
>   The saintly veil of maiden white to throw,
> Confounded, that her maker's eyes
> Should look so near upon her foul deformities.   (29–44)

---

[7] Similarly, in Milton's first English poem, 'On the Death of a Fair Infant Dying of a Cough', despite the very specific title, there is nothing very much like a cough or even an infant in the poem.

As we will see more, Milton's tendency is to make abstract concepts concrete: like Shakespeare, he wants to give 'to aery nothing / A local habitation and a name' (*A Midsummer Night's Dream*, 5.1.16–17). Here Milton is essentially setting the scene, saying, 'it is winter', a time when nature is stripped down and bleak. But this picture is far from the simplicity and ease of conventional Christmas carols. By speaking in this elaborate and indirect way, giving nature the form of a naked female figure, Milton foregrounds the background, so that it moment-arily takes over the story. In fact, the personification of nature in lines 29–34 generates a short scene in 35–44 which takes us away not only from the baby but from the actual landscape itself. Nature is repre-sented as oddly *unnatural*, turned into an allegorical character who is also intensely self-conscious and scrambles to hide 'her naked shame, / Pollute with sinful blame' (40–1). The barrenness of December seems now no longer simply a neutral physical fact but a sign of the world's sinfulness.

There is something rather prudish, even 'puritanical' is this scene, that seems strange for a Milton who in *Paradise Lost* will ostentatiously celebrate Adam's and Eve's nudity, and denounce hypocritical 'Puritans' who think there is anything wrong with the naked human body that God designed (*Paradise Lost* 4.739–75). The specific image of the 'veil' that Nature uses to cover herself suggests the logic of the imagery here. The descent of Christ to earth is a moment of revela-tion, showing the divine in the mortal. We tend, however, to think of revelation, a word derived from the Latin *velum*, veil, as an *un*veiling, a stripping off of false appearances to get at the 'naked' truth (as implied in the last book of the Bible, the Book of Revelation). So William Blake famously dreamed of removing all the illusions that block us from seeing reality: 'If the doors of perception were cleansed every thing would appear to man as it is, infinite. For man has closed him-self up, till he sees all things thro' narrow chinks of his cavern.'[8] But Milton makes the moment of revelation a literal *re*-veiling and cloth-ing of the world, as Christ 'puts on' human flesh. The incarnation is thus also like poetry, which in medieval and Renaissance theory was commonly described with images of veils or clothing. The scene

[8] 'The Marriage of Heaven and Hell', *Blake: Complete Writings*, ed. Geoffrey Keynes (London: Oxford University Press, 1976), 148–60, 154.

introduces and explains Milton's indirect and excessive poetics: the divine can be represented only through the images and scenes which also paradoxically hide it from us. Poetic representation is not a process of stripping off veils but one of putting them on, as the poet uses language and imagery to 'incarnate' the truth. Christianity thus helps Milton answer Plato: while for Plato and his followers the idea that art cloaks nature is suspect, suggesting duplicity and the concealment of the truth, Milton's truth is only revealed by being concealed in poetic images, in the same way that God is revealed when he is embodied as man.

As God redeems the world by taking on a human form, poetry remakes it by putting ideas and feelings into images. The poem is itself a kind of incarnation, as Milton links what happens on the first Christmas day, when the divine becomes human, and what is happening on Christmas day 1629 when he writes the poem. As an indirect means of thinking about what poetry does, he asks us to think about what really happens at the incarnation: what does Christ's descent into a human body *do*, how does it change the world? What difference does it make to us, especially given that our world is still sinful? Milton's contemporaries would have of course *believed* in the incarnation, which is a central part of Christian doctrine, but that is not always the same as *thinking* about it. In fact, as Milton was well aware, doctrine can discourage examination: believers can be called on to have faith and asked not to try to unravel God's mysteries. Like many of the more radical Protestants, Milton rejected the blind following of traditions and church dogma, insisting that each individual must interpret the scripture for him and herself. Yet he was at the same time aware also of the powerful allure of abnegating the heavy burden of interpretation.[9] If the cozy familiarity of belief can at times impede us

---

[9] Already in *Areopagitica* (1644) Milton worries that there are people who don't want to be bothered with thinking about difficult subjects and are quite happy to let others do their thinking for them: 'Another sort there be who, when they hear that all things shall be ordered, all things regulated and settled [by the government],...will straight give themselves up into your hands, make 'em and cut 'em out what religion ye please. There be delights, there be recreations and jolly pastimes that will fetch the day about from sun to sun, and rock the tedious year as in a delightful dream. What need they torture their heads with that which others have taken so strictly and so unalterably into their own purveying? These are the fruits which a dull ease and cessation of our knowledge will bring forth among the people' (Kerrigan, 953). I'll return to this in Chapter 3.

from experiencing the outrageousness of what is happening here, Milton wants poetry to help us recover its deep wonder.

It may therefore be easier for readers today who see Christianity as a foreign mythology to seize the strangeness of the very idea of the incarnation that Milton explores in this poem.[10] One of the unique features of Christianity, the idea that God became human in the form of Jesus Christ is perhaps the ultimate paradox. While Platonic thought especially assumes a fundamental gap between the divine and human, the spiritual and earthly, the incarnation insists that they are opposites that can be united in one form. God can be both transcendent and immanent, spiritual and earthly, omnipotent and a helpless baby. For Milton, the idea of God's descent is an exhilarating but challenging concept, one with which he wrestles throughout his life.[11] The poem shows how difficult it is to imagine an all-powerful God who can become human—not just an infant, but a man who suffers and then *dies* on the cross. It defies logic. The concept of the crucifixion—the death of God—is especially shocking for Milton. In the 'Nativity Ode', he can barely face the little baby, and when he does, he tends to swerve wildly from images of weakness to those of strength. In the Book of Revelation, it is prophesied that Christ will return in the future, now not as a helpless child but as an omnipotent judge, who will reward the good and punish the bad, and re-establish paradise on earth. Milton jumps to this point in Christ's story at every opportunity:

[10] Readers familiar with Graeco-Roman mythology might find in such myths a contrasting model for how gods can take on human forms in order to rape and destroy mortals. In the classical tradition, any kind of 'incarnation' does not unite the divine and the human but reinforces the hierarchical relation in which the former preys on the latter.

[11] In a theological treatise Milton worked on throughout his life, he asserted fervently that he believed that God and man unite in the incarnation. However, while calling it 'the greatest mystery of our religion', he admitted that 'We do not know how it is so, and it is best for us to be ignorant of things which God wishes to remain secret' (*Christian Doctrine*; Kerrigan, 1254, 1256). Although Milton avoided trying to explain this mystery, poetic language allows him to imagine it indirectly. The challenge of representing how the divine can become human has appealed to many literary and visual artists, who also used the subject to capture the tension between the earthly and the transcendent and indeed show the transcendent in the earthly. The simple and down-to-earth drawings by Raphael of the infant Jesus thus commonly present the baby squirming to break free from his mother's arms: he is both a child, bound to a mother who wants to nurse and protect him, and God, set aside from her by his absolute otherness.

> The babe lies yet in smiling infancy,
> That on the bitter cross
> Must redeem our loss;
>   So both himself and us to glorify:
> Yet first to those ychained in sleep,
> The wakeful trump of doom must thunder through the deep.
>
> With such a horrid clang
> As on Mount Sinai rang
>   While the red fire, and smold'ring clouds out brake:
> The agèd earth aghast
> With terror of that blast,
>   Shall from the surface to the center shake;
> When at the world's last session,
> The dreadful judge in middle air shall spread his throne.   (151–64)

Looking at the newborn baby in line 151 makes Milton immediately think of his future death in 152–3, from which he rushes to the future scene of the Last Judgement which he elaborates with some enthusiasm as a spectacular shaking up of the universe (155–64). It seems easier, maybe safer, for Milton to imagine God as 'The dreadful judge' than as a helpless baby. The poem shows his struggle to find a language that can express the paradoxical and unsettling union of absolute power and powerlessness.

The poem's jumbling of past, present, and future shows another consequence of the incarnation, however, that challenges the young poet. Conventional chronology breaks down when eternity enters the world of time. Everything seems to happen at once as the two Christmas days meet. To complicate things further, the incarnation reminds Milton of the creation scene in Genesis, as the song the angels sing at Christ's birth is the same heard when God made the world:

> Such music (as 'tis said)
> Before was never made,
>   But when of old the sons of morning sung,
> While the Creator great
> His constellations set,
>   And the well-balanced world on hinges hung,
> And cast the dark foundations deep,
> And bid the welt'ring waves their oozy channel keep.   (117–24)

The creation of the world at the beginning of time, the birth of Christ, and Milton's writing of the poem in 1629, all seem to come together to form one continuous act of making the universe that leads to an apocalypse now, as Milton cries:

Ring out ye crystal spheres...

For if such holy song
Enwrap our fancy long,
　Time will run back, and fetch the age of gold,
And speckled Vanity
Will sicken soon and die,
　And lep'rous Sin will melt from earthly mold,
And Hell itself will pass away,
And leave her dolorous mansions to the peering day.

Yea Truth and Justice then
Will down return to men,
　Orbed in a rainbow; and, like glories wearing,
Mercy will sit between,
Throned in celestial sheen,
　With radiant feet the tissued clouds down steering,
And Heav'n as at some festival,
Will open wide the gates of her high palace hall.　(125, 133–48)

Time moves in two opposite directions at once as the incarnation makes it 'run back' to the golden age of Eden but also run forward to the future, when hell will dissolve and Eden will be restored on earth.

However, when the poem leaps towards the future it is held back by a greater force: 'But *wisest Fate* says no, / This must not yet be so, / The babe lies yet in smiling infancy' (149–51; emphasis added). The apocalypse is still far off; the baby has just been born and must go through his life in the normal temporal sequence. Milton himself must learn to be patient. As this example shows, Milton frequently imagines restraint as a higher authority outside of himself to which he must submit against his will, though ultimately for his own benefit. The most famous example of this is probably in 'Sonnet 19' on his blindness, in which the speaker first complains that his blindness prevents him from serving God. He is stopped by the figure of 'patience' (8) who jumps in and reassures him by telling him that his inactivity is itself active service: 'They also serve who only stand and wait' (14).

Similarly, the figure of Fate here intervenes and keeps him from getting ahead of himself by pulling him back into the present.

But poetic form itself also holds back the ambitious young poet, offering him a vital means of self-restraint that proves paradoxically liberating for the poet. The inventive and complex form of the 'Nativity Ode' both displays Milton's ambitions and checks them. There are two distinct parts, each written in different metrical patterns. The opening four stanzas are based on the traditional measured and stately form of rhyme royal: seven iambic pentameter lines (five short/long feet) organized in an ABABBCC rhyme scheme. Rhyme *royal* seems generally appropriate for the King of Kings; moreover, originating with Chaucer and his followers and still popular with the Elizabethans, it allows Milton to place himself in a native tradition as he begins his career. The form also suits this subject. Here is the first stanza:

> This is the month, and this the happy morn　　A
> Wherein the Son of Heav'n's eternal King,　　B
> Of wedded maid, and virgin mother born,　　A
> Our great redemption from above did bring;　B
> For so the holy sages once did sing,　　　　B
> 　　That he our deadly forfeit should release,　C
> And with his Father work us a perpetual peace.　C
> 　　　　　　　　　　　　　　　　　(1–7)

I'm emphasizing the rhyme scheme here, as we too often think of rhyme as itself somewhat superfluous, a source of delight but not essential to meaning. For Milton, however, the patterns of rhyme themselves embody the paradoxes at the heart of the poem and the incarnation itself. Note how each stanza is made up of two opening interlocking couplets (ABAB) followed by two rhyming couplets (BBCC). There is a sudden turn from one pattern (ABAB) to the next (BBCC) in the middle of the stanza when the pivotal B that completes the first interlocking couplet now begins and becomes part of a new set of rhyming couplets. This means, moreover, that paradoxically the seven lines are arranged in two intersecting sets of four lines each—ABABBCC—as if they were in fact eight lines. *Seven*, the number of days of the week and so suggesting time, contains *eight*, a number traditionally associated with eternity. The sense of a form going beyond itself is also encouraged by Milton's slight variation on rhyme royal: he gives the last line of each stanza an extra foot, as if the stanzas were also striving to break formal limits and reach beyond time to eternity. However, even as the poem seems to push forward it pulls back. The opening interlocking couplets (ABAB) propel the verse onward, creating a sense of movement. We have to move beyond the unit of the couplet to complete the sound and look forward to see how it will end: to find the 'born' (3) that answers the 'morn' (1). But at the centre of each stanza the pattern, and indeed tempo, changes as the extra B surprises us, stopping us briefly as we change direction and moving us into a new pattern of rhyming couplets (BBCC). In this part, the completion of the sound every second line with the rhyming couplet slows things down for a moment, reining in the poet's energy. The end stopping of lines and almost complete lack of enjambment in this section of the poem (the exceptions are lines 15–16 and 22–3) also helps slow the tempo further. While the incarnation and Milton's poetry take us out of time, the poem reminds us that poetry moves through time, depending essentially on the control of time and tempo for its meaning.

The relation between movement and rest changes but is equally intricate in the second part of the poem, called 'The Hymn'. Milton suddenly abandons rhyme royal, breaking free from tradition and taking up a completely new and original form, as if he now feels he must create something unprecedented to embody this unprecedented event. While the stanzas in the first part of the poem are organized into seven-line units that act as if they were eight lines, those of the second part are actually eight lines. The new stanzas are made up of two short iambic trimeter couplets (three short/long feet) followed by a pentameter (five short/long feet), ending with a final couplet that joins one tetrameter line (four short/long feet) and a longer closing hexameter (six short/long feet). The overall pattern thus looks like this:

It was the winter wild,	A^3
While the Heav'n-born-child,	A^3
All meanly wrapped in the rude manger lies;	$\mathbf{B}^5$
Nature in awe to him	C^3
Had doffed her gaudy trim	C^3
With her great master so to sympathize:	$\mathbf{B}^5$
It was no season then for her	D^4
To wanton with the sun her lusty paramour.	D^6

(29–36)

As in rhyme royal, it is the B that is the wild card, disrupting the pattern that the first couplets tempt us to expect and sending us off in a new direction. One might think of this also as a hybrid form in which three rhyming couplets (AA CC DD) are interrupted by one envelope rhyme (BCCB) which balances and binds the three parts of the poem like this: *AA*B *CC* B*DD* (wild/child/**lies**/*him*/*trim*/ **sympathize**/her/paramour). But the binding is not tight, as the central envelope rhyme (BCCB) stands apart from the opening and closing couplets. In other ways too it seems a less settled form than that of the poised and regal rhyme royal. Where in rhyme royal the lines are all of equal length, five feet, here the variation, and the more frequent use of enjambment, creates a pulsating rhythm of expansion and contraction, a simultaneous reaching forward and pulling back. Visually, the unevenness of line lengths, including that of the final couplet which joins unequal feet, reminds us of the gap between the human and the divine even as the two are brought together.

I have drawn such close attention to Milton's use of form here because the poem insists that meaning is incarnated in language just as God is in human flesh. Milton is showing what poetry can do, and how it offers an expanded way of knowing the world, giving precise shape and form to abstract ideas. With its ability to say two contradictory things and indeed move in two directions at once, its existence in time and push towards time's transcendence, poetry can represent the radical event of an incarnation which joins two natures. It can show us the mystery of the divine in the human.

This double vision is expressed not only in the structure of the poem, with its two sections of distinct but hybrid metrical patterns, but also in the tension between the Christian subject and a surprising amount of pagan imagery. Most extravagant, and indeed superfluous to the supposed subject, is the section in stanzas 19–26 in which Milton draws on an ancient belief that when Christ was born, the classical gods were driven from the earth: 'The Oracles are dumb, / No voice or hideous hum / Runs through the archèd roof in words deceiving' (173–5). In these eight stanzas, Milton represents how the incarnated Word of God exposes the falsity of the old 'deceiving' (175) classical myths which now should be abandoned for the one truth. For Christians, the story of Christ's birth, death, and resurrection is not a fiction or mere 'myth'; it actually happened in human history and is therefore far superior to classical fables. Many seventeenth-century English poets were concerned with separating pagan lies from Christian truth to create a pure Christian poetics. They saw myths as idolatrous and unscientific holdovers from a world of ancient superstition that had been superseded by first Christianity and then modern science.[12] Writing poems about salacious pagan gods, whose descents to earth wreak havoc and destruction, seemed unseemly and childish for a mature nation governed by Christian and scientific truths.

Moreover, by dividing the false myths of the pagan past from the true stories inspired by the Word, seventeenth-century writers were able to offer a spirited response to the perennial attacks on poetry, and those of Plato in particular. The 'Nativity Ode' seems to head in this direction when it makes the incarnation the beginning of a new, true because Christian, poetics, which silences the false poetry of classical myths. But despite Milton's claim that the gods are struck 'dumb', these deities are hardly silent; they go out with a lot of weeping and wailing and gnashing of teeth. At the very moment that Milton seems to proclaim that these gods are not real, he gives them reality, by fleshing them out. The long description of their leaving is excessive: Apollo shrieks loudly as he is forced to leave his temple at Delphi (176–80), while all of nature mourns the tragic loss of great powers emptying the world:

> The lonely mountains o'er,
> And the resounding shore,
>   A voice of weeping heard, and loud lament;
> From haunted spring, and dale
> Edged with poplar pale,
>   The parting Genius is with sighing sent;
> With flow'r-inwoven tresses torn,
> The Nymphs in twilight shade of tangled thickets mourn.   (181–8)

---

[12] So Abraham Cowley, a contemporary poet Milton admired, claimed that 'It is time to recover it [poetry] out of the *Tyrants* hands, and to restore it to the *Kingdom* of *God*, who is the *Father* of it. It is time to *Baptize* it in *Jordan*, for it will never become clean by bathing in the *Water* of *Damascus*.' In *Abraham Cowley: Poems; Miscellanies, The Mistress, Pindarique Odes, Davideis, Verses Written on Several Occasions*, ed. A. R. Waller (Cambridge: Cambridge University Press, 1905), 12–13.

Milton lets us feel the imaginative power of the classical tradition even as it is put in its place in his Christian poetics. Classical myths don't need to be excluded completely if they can be controlled by the poet in the same way that the old gods are by the baby who 'Can in his swaddling bands control the damnèd crew' (228). Old lies can be harnessed to tell a new truth.

It's not just the old gods that need controlling, however. The containment of the gods in 'th' infernal jail' (233) is the climax of a pattern of the restraining and channelling of energy that began with the covering of Nature. With the old myths now under control, the poem returns at last to the real subject to bring itself to an end:

> But see the virgin blest,
> Hath laid her babe to rest.
>   Time is our tedious song should here have ending:
> Heav'n's youngest teemèd star,
> Hath fixed her polished car,
>   Her sleeping Lord with handmaid lamp attending:
> And all about the courtly stable,
> Bright-harnessed angels sit in order serviceable.   (237–44)

We return finally to the nativity scene, and the sleeping baby. While 'Bright-*harnessed*' might recall the more conventional donkeys and oxen we might well expect to see, Milton's stable is full not of animals but angels. Their harnesses also suggest that while the false gods need to be jailed, even these good angels need to be reined in—though *they* get nice shiny harnesses. The ambitious young poet himself, eager to get ahead, also needs to be harnessed, restrained through the binding power of rhyme and the story of Christ. It is hard not to think that Milton has snuck himself into the scene as part of the angelic order; perhaps he is 'Heav'n's youngest-teemèd star', who attaches his polished poem to the Son who is the invisible and yet omnipotent origin of all creative energy. He has found the subject, source, and model for his poetry and is going to fix himself to it as closely as possible. The sleeping Word made flesh is the silent and concealed centre of creative power, an alpha and omega that both generates the poem and then brings it full circle to conclude. The tiny baby who can 'control the damnèd crew' (228) is not so helpless after all. The image of Christ, complemented by the restrictions of poetic form itself, helps

Milton restrain and channel his own poetic powers. The story of the omnipotent God who surrenders all power but will ultimately recover it when he returns as judge at the last day reassures Milton about his own decision to make himself vulnerable by putting off worldly success in favour of writing. What looks like weakness and restriction can be a form of strength and freedom.

First Endings: 'Lycidas'

The beginning of the 1645 *Poems* shows that Christ makes Milton a poet, giving him not only his subject but his source of inspiration. It marks Milton's own creative birth. The series of English poems concludes with a poem about death not birth, endings rather than beginnings, and brings to an end the story of poetic and personal development begun in the 'Nativity Ode'.

'Lycidas', an elegy written in 1637 for a memorial volume for a fellow Cambridge student, Edward King, who had drowned in a shipwreck, laments the premature end of a young man of promise, someone rather like Milton himself. It is the culmination of Milton's early training in writing funeral elegies. But as Milton has grown up, what was once a mere exercise is starting to become something more real. 'Lycidas' looks forward to Milton's treatment of loss and alienation in *Paradise Lost*. A new consciousness of the reality of death brings about a kind of fall from innocence as death transforms the natural world from an idyllic garden to a hostile jungle:

> But O the heavy change, now thou art gone,
> Now thou art gone, and never must return!
> Thee shepherd, thee the woods, and desert caves,
> With wild thyme and the gadding vine o'ergrown,
> And all their echoes mourn.   (37–41)

In the 'Nativity Ode', the coming of Christ filled and completed nature, giving it shape and meaning. Now, death empties and strips it, revealing to the poet its hostile meaninglessness. Disillusioned, the speaker now sees the fertile luxury of the Eden of his youth as sterile, self-destructive excess of overgrowth. Milton is facing a crisis of confidence about his choice of writing as a meaningful way to spend his life. While the 'Nativity Ode' asks how to begin writing, 'Lycidas' faces the question of how and why to go on in the face of knowledge of mortality. Poetry is supposed to make sense of death and offer consolation; now, however, just when death starts to become real, poetry seems unreal and useless. Poetry does nothing: the poem remembers that the first poet, Orpheus, who tried and failed to conquer death with his song, was himself killed brutally (57–63). Perhaps the Puritans were right after all.

'Lycidas' is a poem about breaking, the sudden and premature rupture of a human life, that makes Milton question his decision to be a poet. The speaker claims that he writes against his own will, and is forced by 'Bitter constraint, and sad occasion dear' (6), the abrupt shattering of Edward King's life, to 'Shatter' (5) nature. Specifically, he tears up the three kinds of leaves—the laurel, myrtle, and ivy— that are entwined in the poet's laurel crown, suggesting his bitter renunciation of his poetic aspirations. If the 'Nativity Ode' is pulled in two directions, rushing forward to heaven and pulling itself back to earth, 'Lycidas' is all over the place, suggesting the poet's loss of direction. G. Wilson Knight described the poem beautifully as 'an effort to bind and clamp together a universe trying to fly off into separate bits; it is an accumulation of magnificent fragments'.[13] It is as if the sudden shocking consciousness of the brutality of the world, nature's cold indifference to human suffering, has put such pressure on the conventional ways of controlling and shaping grief that both poet and poem fall to pieces. Nothing seems adequate. The honesty of the poem is heart-breaking.

Reflecting a world that seems to have fallen apart, 'Lycidas' is not divided into stanzas that might give it an underlying unifying pattern. Although rhyme normally creates a sense of predictability, the scheme here is unpredictable and the poem seems to break down into a series of rather disjointed sections, fragments from different poetic traditions, as if Milton were trying out different poetic avenues to see where they lead him but then abandoning each in despair as it only brings him to a dead end. Tradition as a whole now has been exposed

---

[13] See *Poets of Action: Incorporating Essays from the 'Burning Oracle'*, reprint (London: Methuen, 1967), 28. Knight's reading originally published in 1939 reflects the context in which it was written: WWII, with its devastating decimation of young men and sense that the world was indeed being blown apart.

as an empty shell, unable to answer the questions the poet raises. The poem keeps starting, stopping, and restarting; Milton can't be sure of where he is going because Edward King's death calls into question the plans for a future that may in fact never take place. Since the poet also might die young, why should he struggle to write?

> Alas! What boots it with uncessant care
> To tend the homely slighted shepherd's trade,
> And strictly meditate the thankless muse?
> Were it not better done as others use,
> To sport with Amaryllis in the shade,
> Or with the tangles of Neaera's hair?   (64–9)

Why not just have fun? Apollo, the classical god of poetry, gives the classical response to this problem: the dead live on through their good deeds, commemorated in poetry (76–84). Poetry's purpose is to keep the dead alive. While that is the answer of Milton's earlier elegies and the claim of 'To His Father', it has lost its reassurance here, and now appears potentially a self-deluding and superficial consolation: 'to interpose a little ease, / Let our frail thoughts dally with false surmise' (152–3). It seems as if poetry is simply 'false surmise': all it can do is offer us comforting but escapist fictions that we can 'dally' with for a 'little' temporary 'ease' from the harshness of reality.

In the 'Nativity Ode', Apollo is one of the banished gods, whose 'words deceiving' ('Nativity Ode' 175) are supplanted by the true Word. Here too, the figure of Christ replaces the god of poetry as well as the poet Orpheus as a model for poetry itself, bringing the poem to an end and helping the poet find a new sense of direction and purpose. The general structure follows the conventional pattern of the early elegies in which Milton asserts that the dead live on in heaven. Death is not an end but a beginning; the poem turns abruptly one last time to set out in a completely new direction. Rupture is transformed into a positive force, one that frees the poet and lets him break away from the cycle of grief:

> Weep no more, woeful shepherds, weep no more,
> For Lycidas your sorrow is not dead,
> Sunk though he be beneath the wat'ry floor,
> So sinks the day-star in the ocean bed,
> And yet anon repairs his drooping head,

And tricks his beams, and with new-spangled ore,
Flames in the forehead of the morning sky:
So Lycidas sunk low, but mounted high,
Through the dear might of him that walked the waves.   (165–73)

There are two central images for rebirth here, however, and they are slightly at odds with each other. The first (168–71) is drawn from nature: in imagining the resurrection of Lycidas in heaven, Milton finds an obvious analogue in the sun, 'the day-star', as it sinks at night and then rises again each morning. But the natural cyclical resurrection of the sun is not, alas, really an appropriate image for human beings. When flowers die they are reborn each year; humans are not. So in his version of 'Lycidas', 'Adonais', written for Keats, Shelley rails against the injustice that 'Nought we know, dies. Shall that alone which knows / Be as a sword consumed before the sheath / By sightless lightning?' (177–9).[14] From the start of Milton's poem, the speaker is aware that human consciousness and especially the knowledge of mortality alienates him irrevocably from the natural world of endlessly repeated cycles. Humans are not one with nature. The solution thus has to come from a supernatural source, and in 172–3, the poem turns to Christ, the one truth whom classical figures like Apollo and Orpheus merely copy, and the guarantor of spiritual rebirth and immortality.

To reach such a conclusion many Christian poets would have immediately thought of Christ's passion, his death on the cross that leads to his resurrection. As I've suggested, however, Milton seems to find the idea of God's death too disturbing to be entertained for long; it does not offer him the reassurance he needs. In general, he stays away from that scene to focus on other moments in Christ's life. Here, he remembers a famous story in the gospels in which Christ showed his divinity by walking on the sea of Galilee (Matthew 14:22–36; Mark 6:45–56; John 6:16–21). On a basic level, the specific representation of Christ here marks the speaker's detachment from identification with the drowned Edward King, who was 'Sunk...beneath the wat'ry floor' (167), and his alignment instead with 'him that walked the waves' (173).

[14] *Shelley: Poetical Works*, ed. Thomas Hutchinson (Oxford: Oxford University Press, 1970), 436.

But Christ's power over water is not just arbitrary proof of his supernatural powers or his difference from King. Control of water is a traditional biblical image for divine creativity, beginning in Genesis when 'the Spirit of God moved upon the face of the waters' (Genesis 1:2) to make the world. So in the 'Nativity Ode' Milton describes how at the original creation God bid the 'welt'ring waves their oozy channel keep' (124).[15] When Christ walks on water he re-enacts this primal moment; in the 'Nativity Ode', Milton makes the moment of incarnation itself a re-making of the world:

> But peaceful was the night
> Wherein the Prince of Light
> His reign of peace upon the earth began:
> The Winds with wonder whist,
> Smoothly the waters kissed,
> Whispering new joys to the mild Ocean,
> Who now hath quite forgot to rave,
> While birds of calm sit brooding on the charmèd wave.   (61–8)

Milton will use the image of the bird hovering over water later in *Paradise Lost* 1.20–2, when he describes how in making the world the Spirit of God 'with mighty wings outspread / Dove-like sat'st brooding on the vast abyss / And mad'st it pregnant'. Divine creation is symbolized as movement over water. In an England newly aspiring to imperial status, however, control over water was also becoming a symbol of national power; as the famous eighteenth-century song goes, 'Britannia rules the waves'. God is indeed an Englishman. The image had become especially resonant for English poets in the late 1500s when Edmund Spenser represented himself as the poet who 'tuned it [his song] unto the waters' fall' ('April Eclogue' 36).[16] Book Four of his epic romance *The Faerie Queene* ends with a long list of all the names of the rivers in England, in which Spenser proudly showed

---

[15] The water imagery links the two poems that frame the beginning and end of this section of the 1645 *Poems*. The language 'And bid the *welt'r*ing waves their *oozy* channel keep' ('Nativity Ode' 124) reappears in 'Lycidas' when the speaker fears that Lycidas' body may '*welter* to the parching wind' (13) and later when the drowning is reimagined as a baptism in which 'With nectar pure his *oozy* locks he laves' (175; all emphases added).

[16] *The Poetical Works of Edmund Spenser: In Three Volumes*, Vol. 1: *Spenser's Minor Poems*, ed. Ernest De Selincourt (Oxford: Oxford University Press, 1910); spelling slightly modernized.

he could turn water into magnificent poetry. Writers following Spenser, including Milton, used the image of poetic control of water to assert their own claim to speak for an island nation. The British poet also rules the waves, harnessing the fluidity and energy of both water and poetry itself.[17]

While the figure of Christ recalls the resurrection, the image of walking on water identifies him specifically with a creative, and especially English, energy. Christ embodies the primal force of creation that puts the poet and poem back together. Poetry matters because it is an expression of a creativity that to Milton takes us beyond the limitations of our own finite selves that end all too soon. At the end of the poem, the ruptured world gains a new form in the pure creative act itself. The speaker recovers a sense of forward momentum with a sudden surge of confidence:

> Thus sang the uncouth swain to th' oaks and rills,
> While the still Morn went out with sandals gray;
> He touched the tender stops of various quills,
> With eager thought warbling his Doric lay:
> And now the sun had stretched out all the hills,
> And now was dropped into the western bay;
> At last he rose, and twitched his mantle blue:
> Tomorrow to fresh woods, and pastures new.   (186–93)

The shift from first to third person shows the speaker separating himself from an earlier version of himself (now suddenly imagined in the past tense as an 'uncouth swain') to move on as a poet and person. The poem charts Milton's symbolic death, as he begins a new stage of personal and poetic development. What looked like a premature ending becomes a new beginning. The formally erratic poem settles into an identifiable rhyme scheme: the eight-line ottava rima (ABABABCC) which was the metre of Italian epic. The poet now can go on toward a tomorrow and pastures new that will include his own epic, *Paradise*

---

[17] Keats's famous epitaph 'Here lies One whose Name was writ in Water' is thus more complex than usually assumed, implying both the feared ephemerality of his poetry and its power and endurance. There are of course different kinds of bodies of water that are all very important in England—rivers, lakes, and oceans—and which poets can use to define and differentiate themselves from other poets. Thus the second-generation Romantics found the '*Lake* Poets' too tame, and took as their source of inspiration the sea; see especially Byron, *Childe Harold's Pilgrimage* 4.179, 184.

Lost. If the 1645 *Poems* show Milton's development as a poet, they also suggest the deepening of his understanding of what poetry can do and what kind of poet he will be.

The Truth of Masks[18]

> the truest poetry is the most feigning.
>
> Shakespeare, *As You Like It* 3.3.19–20

The Milton I have been discussing so far is a very serious young man, who takes himself, and being a poet, very seriously. He is a devout Christian, who sees his poetics as inspired by and continuous with the creativity expressed through Christ's incarnation. To become a poet, he remarks later, requires years of careful disciplined study of all aspects of human experience: 'industrious and select reading, steady observation, insight into all seemly and generous arts and affairs' (*The Reason of Church Government*, 1642; Kerrigan, 843). He believes that a poet should be held to high standards of behaviour, and should have tremendous powers of self-restraint, sublimating sexual desire into his art. Unlike almost every other poet of the time, he resists the pressure to write the kind of secular love poetry popular at the time, known best today probably through the works of John Donne. Arranging his poems in the 1645 volume, he followed the 'Nativity Ode' with some more religious poems on other days in the liturgical calendar as well as some translations of the Psalms.

But the collection also contains lighter pieces: poems celebrating the coming of spring, the power of music, friendship, and even love. There are some comic elegies on the death of the University carrier (i.e. porter) which treat death wittily, and satiric Latin poems on the Gunpowder Plot. While his poem 'Il Penseroso' celebrates a life of restraint, discipline, and the contemplation of higher things, its companion poem 'L'Allegro' offers an equally attractive life of carefree 'heart-easing Mirth' (13) in a world of 'sunshine holiday' (98). Milton's original spelling of holiday as holyday is telling, suggesting that such free recreation is not empty-headed frivolity but indeed 'holy'.

---

[18] The title of one of Wilde's great critical essays; see *Complete Works*, 1060.

As we saw in 'Sonnet 20', Milton valued highly friendship, good wine, music (he was an excellent musician), and conversation as essential to a meaningful and fully human life. In a university debate on the topic 'Sportive Exercises on occasion are not inconsistent with philosophical Studies', he had argued against the kind of either/or thinking encouraged by such debates, and especially the antithesis between levity and gravity. He pointed out that deep writers and thinkers such as Homer and Socrates and moralists like Cato had playful sides and enjoyed timely recreation; even the gods fool around. Being silly is a serious business, as 'no one can be master of a fine and clever wit who has not yet first learnt how to behave seriously'.[19] While it is always unwise to take a school assignment as an expression of Milton's beliefs, the argument seems to have resonated with him. Writing both the joyfully bouncy 'L'Allegro' and the more solemn and contemplative 'Il Penseroso' showed that the poet can and indeed must be both.

The need to find a place for pleasure in serious poetry is at the very centre of the 1645 *Poems*. Although 'Lycidas' seems to mark the end of a stage in the young poet's development, it was not in fact the last English work in his first collection. It was followed by a very different kind of writing: a drama, entitled *A Mask*, though commonly known as *Comus* (the name I will use here) after its compelling villain. Coming after 'Lycidas' and preceding the second half of Latin poems, *Comus* is the heart of the volume and seems to draw together its major themes. At the same time, it stands out from the other early works both for its genre and for its length: at 1023 lines, it shows Milton's eagerness to move on from the small poems appropriate for a young poet to something bigger and more demanding. While *Comus* is a dramatic work, its basic plot is a version of a classic epic quest familiar in works from the *Odyssey* through Spenser's *Faerie Queene* to *The Wizard of Oz*. The story is classic: trying to get home to their parents through a forest, its heroes, the young Lady and her two brothers, are impeded by an evil enchanter, Comus, who has the power to turn humans into half-animal forms, and helped by a good Attendant Spirit sent from heaven, along with a water spirit, Sabrina. In its themes of trial and temptation the play seems in many ways a rehearsal of *Paradise Lost*.

[19] See 'Prolusion Six' in the *Complete Prose Works* 1:276.

Like so many of Milton's works, *Comus* revolves around debates. The two brothers argue over the Lady's safety in 331–480, and the climax of the work is a verbal duel between Comus and the Lady in 659–813. Repeatedly divided into opposing points of view, the world of the poem seems rather doggedly du*e*listic and du*a*listic, split essentially into the moral categories of good and evil, virtue and vice. At the start, the two sides are identified with the spirit and the flesh, as they often are, especially in Platonic or Neoplatonic thought. Heaven and earth, the spiritual world above and the material world below, are starkly contrasted, as the Elder Brother imagines a bifurcated world in which the good are turned 'by degrees to the soul's essence, / Till all be made immortal' (462–3), while the soul of a sinner is 'clotted by contagion', which 'Embodies and imbrutes, till she quite lose / The divine property of her first being' (467–9). The good rise up to heaven to become pure spirit while the bad sink down to earth to undergo a kind of anti-incarnation in which they are 'imbruted'.

The central figures of the innocent and chaste Lady and the lustful and carnal Comus incarnate this opposition between heaven and earth, virtue and sensual pleasure, truth/reality and falsehood/illusion. As I noted earlier, moreover, for Milton chastity is connected to his thinking about poetry: sexual continence is essential for the poet who wants himself to be a 'true poem' (*An Apology for Smectymnuus*, 1642; Kerrigan, 850). Moral opposites, the two central characters embody also alternative arguments about what poetry does, how it does it, and where it leads us. When Comus hears the Lady's singing he is struck with wonder. While it reminds him of the enchanting song of his mother, the classical witch Circe, he recognizes the crucial difference between the two types of music:

> they in pleasing slumber lulled the sense,
> And in sweet madness robbed it of itself,
> But such a sacred and home-felt delight,
> Such sober certainty of waking bliss
> I never heard till now.   (260–4)

Both the songs of the Lady and of Circe are beautiful and powerful, but they do opposite things: the Lady's chaste song wakes its listeners up to the truth, while Circe's sensual one lulls its unsuspecting audience to sleep with pleasant falsehoods. The fact that the Lady's song brings 'home-felt delight' recalls broadly Neoplatonic accounts of the soul's descent from and return to its heavenly home. Sent down to earth, the soul yearns to return to its spiritual source but can become ensnared by the illusions of the material world. Such entrapment was identified traditionally with the enchantress Circe who had tried to keep the epic hero Odysseus from getting home. In Milton, Circe's son Comus similarly tries to keep the Lady from achieving her goal with his 'dazzling spells' that are 'Of power to cheat the eye with blear illusion' (154–5). His sensual poetry is dazzling but degrading, leaving his victims lost, stuck in the world of base matter, as through his spells they their 'friends and native home forget / To roll with pleasure in a sensual sty' (76–7). In contrast, the uplifting virginal music of the Lady raises the human to the heavens and so leads them back to their true spiritual home.

The masque thus restages the debate between Gosson and Sidney: Comus confirms Gosson's worst nightmare that the poet is a liar, a depraved seducer who leads us to hell, while the Lady channels Sidney's insistence that the poet reveals the truth and points the way to heaven. At the opening of the masque, the two poetics are distinguished through form. The language of virtue (that of the Lady, her brothers, the Attendant Spirit) is blank verse, the form that Milton will later choose for his epic. I'll say more about this choice in the next chapter, but the use of forms here is crucial in the development of Milton's poetics as he learns further how to use form for dramatic effects and to differentiate speakers. The characters in *Comus* who speak in blank verse are able to debate and present complex ideas. Comus, however, speaks in rhyming iambic tetrameter couplets which create an enchanting musical effect but suggest a potential subordination of sense to sound, the drowning of reason in mere pleasure.

When the Lady arrives, however, Comus switches to blank verse, and so deceives her into going off with him. Evil can easily disguise itself as good. Moreover, the musical speech of Comus is excitingly seductive; the fact that the work is commonly referred to by the name of the villain, rather than that of the heroine, suggests how he charms even readers fully aware that he is a villain. The burden of *Comus*, like other defences of poetry, is to separate good from bad poetry. The debates in the masque offer the conventional method of resolving a problem through logical argumentation leading to a single truth. But debate here proves useless, as Milton suggests the limits of his early training and the kind of thinking it might encourage. Perhaps the young brothers are too eager to apply their school exercises to real life situations, but their tendency to lapse into earnest argument at any opportunity makes them rather hopeless helpers for their sister. Even the vehement debate between the Lady and Comus at the heart of the masque results not in a resolution but in a dead-end. Although Comus recognizes that the Lady is the winner who speaks the truth ('She fables not, I feel that I do fear / Her words set off by some superior power' [800–1]), the truth does not set her free. Their argument leads to a stalemate, in which the two sides seem locked in irresolvable and unproductive opposition; the brothers bungle their attempted rescue, Comus runs off, and the Lady herself is frozen. Rational debate cannot set her free. Poetry, however, can.

The Lady is freed through the help of the Attendant Spirit sent from heaven. His prologue and epilogue, in which he describes his descent from and reascent to heaven, frame the masque. His role recalls that of the epic god Mercury, conventionally sent down from heaven to nudge loitering heroes back on track; in Christian terms, moreover, his descent to save a lost soul recalls the story of Christ. At the start of the masque, he comes from a rather rarefied and abstract heaven of Platonic forms:

> Before the starry threshold of Jove's court
> My mansion is, where those immortal shapes
> Of bright aërial spirits live ensphered
> In regions mild of calm and serene air,
> Above the smoke and stir of this dim spot,
> Which men call earth. (1–6)

This is a rather dry and indeed unpoetic image. Like the brothers, the Spirit imagines the world in black and white terms: calm and serene air versus smoky dim spot. He therefore seems rather unhappy with his mission, fearful lest he 'soil these pure ambrosial weeds / With the rank vapors of this sin-worn mold' (16–17). Platonism and Puritanism meet in this celestial snob who finds his descent from this disembodied realm and his earthly incarnation into the world of ucky matter distasteful and wants to get back up to heaven as quickly as possible. He is less like the Christ who willingly takes on human form than like the Satan of *Paradise Lost* who is disgusted when he makes himself a snake:

> O foul descent! That I who erst contended
> With gods to sit the highest, am now constrained
> Into a beast, and mixed with bestial slime,
> This essence to incarnate and imbrute,
> That to the highth of deity aspired.   (*Paradise Lost* 9.163–7)

For Satan, to be *incarnated* is simply to be *imbruted*.

Yet while the fastidious Spirit starts off eager to finish his mission as quickly as possible and get home for a heavenly shower, he himself delays its completion. With his usual perspicacity, Dr. Johnson first noted something odd about the Lady's rescuers. They talk too much and do too little. Johnson dryly describes what happens after Comus and the Lady leave together (thus just missing the Lady's would-be liberators):

> At last the Brothers enter, with too much tranquillity; and when they have feared lest their sister should be in danger, and hoped that she is not in danger, the Elder makes a speech in praise of chastity, and the Younger finds how fine it is to be a philosopher.
>
> Then descends the Spirit in form of a shepherd; and the Brother, instead of being in haste to ask his help, praises his singing, and enquires his business in that place. It is remarkable, that at this interview the Brother is taken with a short fit of rhyming. The Spirit relates that the Lady is in the power of Comus; the Brother moralises again; and the Spirit makes a long narration, *of no use because it is false, and therefore unsuitable to a good Being.*[20]

The forces that are supposed to propel the plot towards its goal delay it. They are slow and take too much time. Debate itself seems just useless talking, a means of not acting. Johnson thus raises one of the traditional objections to poetry: it distracts us from doing something meaningful and important.

But Johnson's concern goes even deeper. He is especially indignant that when the Spirit, also disguised as a shepherd, finally encounters the boys, he tells them an unnecessarily lengthy and largely made-up

---

[20] 'Life of Milton', 99, emphasis added.

story (540–80) about what has happened. For Johnson this is just plain wrong, as the story is 'false, and therefore unsuitable to a good Being'. How can the agent of truth speak what is not true? But that is precisely the point the Spirit himself has to learn. The language of this fictitious report includes some of the most beautiful poetry in the masque. What the Spirit says is far in excess of what the action requires. To get the job done, all he has to say is essentially, 'They went that-a-way' and then hand the boys the magic flower that can overcome Comus. Instead, he launches into a long, detailed description of how watching his flock he:

> sat me down to watch upon a bank
> With ivy canopied, and interwove
> With flaunting honeysuckle, and began
> Wrapped in a pleasing fit of melancholy
> To meditate my rural minstrelsy
> Till fancy had her fill.   (543–8)

He then says he heard the Lady sing:

> At last a soft and solemn breathing sound
> Rose like a steam of rich distilled perfumes,
> And stole upon the air, that even Silence
> Was took ere she was ware, and wished she might
> Deny her nature, and be never more
> Still to be so displaced. I was all ear,
> And took in strains that might create a soul
> Under the ribs of Death.   (555–62)

It is completely untrue, but it's gorgeous, creating a rich landscape and capturing the feeling of wonder created by the Lady's song—described evocatively as a poetics that 'might create a soul / Under the ribs of Death' (561–2). The lushness of the language here suggests that her music has inspired him too. The care and delicacy with which the Spirit creates the imaginary scene suggest that now, far from being disgusted with his role as he was when he began, he has been caught up in the aesthetic pleasure and beauty of his task. The Spirit's entrance into the world of matter has transformed him from a disembodied figure of virtue into a poet, suddenly sensitive to the beauties of a world he earlier dismissed as simply a 'dim spot' (5).

The Spirit frees the Lady through the further aid of a river goddess, Sabrina. Where the Spirit comes from *above*, Sabrina rises from the waters *below*, suggesting her association with the powers of nature and the material world that are also needed to free the Lady. But Sabrina is not just a force of nature, as her identification with water connects her to the power of poetry. She is an art that both rises from and goes beyond the merely natural. In the end, fictions become the means to truth and bring the Lady home.[21] In the process, moreover, the nature of truth itself is completely transformed. When the Spirit returns to heaven, the arid abstract ideal he spoke of earlier has blossomed into a garden in which:

> Along the crispèd shades and bow'rs
> Revels the spruce and jocund Spring;
> The Graces and the rosy-bosomed Hours,
> Thither all their bounties bring,
> There eternal Summer dwells,
> And west winds with musky wing
> About the cedarn alleys fling
> Nard and Cassia's balmy smells.
> Iris there with humid bow
> Waters the odorous banks that blow
> Flowers of more mingled hue
> Than her purfled scarf can show,
> And drenches with Elysian dew.   (984–96)

The Spirit himself seems to have undergone a change, as he speaks in the bouncy, light-hearted rhyming couplets of Comus. Rhyme, with its enchanting energy, is not inherently evil, and can get us to heaven after all.

But rhyme can also make heaven look quite different. The masque begins in a black and white world but ends in one full of colour. While the Spirit's opening speech chops the universe in half, dividing a pristine heaven *up there* from the dirty world *down here*, his epilogue offers a glimpse of a rich, luxurious, and sensual but spiritual realm, an erotic paradise, full of the 'balmy smells', rainbow (here embodied as Iris)

---

[21] Sabrina is also a figure from a mythic English history whose existence was increasingly questioned at this time and in which Milton expresses little faith in his *History of Britain. Comus* suggests that while the story may be factually false it still holds a *poetic* truth. In this, Sabrina is like the pagan gods in the 'Nativity Ode'.

colours, and sounds of nature. It is a deeply layered world, which at a higher level is inhabited by Venus, classical goddess of love, and her lover Adonis (999–1002). But the myth of Adonis, who is killed by a boar while hunting, was often read as a warning against the danger of desire, a myth that proves that sex is deadly and so should be shunned. The spirit tells us there is another paradise that is even *higher* than that one, one inhabited by Venus' son Cupid, his wife Psyche, and their two children 'Youth and Joy' (1003–11). The goal of the masque is not the banishment of the sensual world by virtue but its elevation to a higher form and truth, a poetic paradise in which a happy marriage of fulfilled and procreative sexual desire is the highest goal and good.

Performed first in 1634, *Comus* was published in a revised form in 1637 and then again in 1645. The original performance opened with a shorter version of what Milton later made the final speech I have cited in part above: a description of a beautiful, sensuous garden. In the early version, however, this landscape was empty, lacking mythical inhabitants or lovers. Perhaps in 1634 Milton wasn't quite ready to imagine people in such a wonderful place. But when Milton published the masque three years later, he wrote the new opening we have now, expanding the original beginning and moving it to the end. The revision makes a big difference, creating a sense of progress: in this new version, the sensual heaven reached through the experience of the poem seems higher and more fulfilling than the abstract vision at the beginning. We can only reach this vision through the poetry itself, as Milton himself had as he wrote and then rewrote his longest early work. In 'To His Father', Milton claimed that poetry can get us to heaven. But *Comus* shows further that reading and writing poetry can change and expand our understanding of what heaven might be. This will be the topic of Milton's great epic, *Paradise Lost*, in which poetic creativity and sexual fulfilment are entwined at the heart of a perfect world.

2

The Poet's Paradise

Reaching for *Paradise Lost*

The 1645 *Poems* show Milton excitedly exploring what poetry can do. But for most of the 1640s and '50s, his poetic development was put almost entirely on hold as he devoted his energies to the political revolution about which he cared deeply. The collapse of the Republic and restoration of the monarchy in 1660 were devastating for him. They might have meant his death. Instead, however, they made him return to the heaven glimpsed at the end of *Comus* and reimagine it as the Garden of Eden of *Paradise Lost*.

Milton probably began writing his epic in the late 1650s, when the totally blind writer had to leave the government position he had held since the overthrow of the monarchy in 1649. Ironically, the loss of sight and, later, the crushing of his political hopes gave him the opportunity to fulfil his early promise and become the poet he had aspired to be. The experiences of war, loss, disability, and political as well as marital disappointment meant, however, that the work Milton finally completed was quite different from what he had originally imagined. Epic in its genre and scope, *Paradise Lost* is also intensely personal, as the older Milton attempts to make sense of the unexpected and often shattering turns of his life and the world around him. It is an astonishing imaginative achievement for a man who might easily have given in to bitterness, self-pity, and despair. Like 'Lycidas', *Paradise Lost* affirms the power of creativity in a world that seems to have fallen apart. For the older Milton, poetry is even more necessary than ever.

It seems inevitable to us today that Milton would have eventually tackled an epic. Any ambitious and serious poet of this time would think of writing such a work. It was seen as the highest literary genre, an encyclopaedia of universal knowledge, and a genre that absorbed all other genres into itself. Such a complex and capacious work stretched its author beyond the limits of his own person, asking him to speak not only for himself but also for his nation, to take on and identify with an entire tradition in order to express the values and history of a people and, beyond that, universal truths. Such work was not to be undertaken lightly or completed quickly. In Milton's time, the chief model for the epic was not Homer, but the Roman poet Virgil, who was said to have first spent three years writing short pastoral poems (*Eclogues*), then seven years on longer pieces (the *Georgics*, a didactic poem on farming), and then devoted eleven years to his great epic, the *Aeneid*. Many later writers felt that like Virgil they had to undergo years of rigorous training and practice to write an epic. The ending of 'Lycidas', with its turn to the ottava rima of Italian epic, might therefore suggest that the 1645 *Poems* was Milton's conscious poetic apprenticeship in which he disciplined himself, mastering a wide range of easier, shorter genres to prepare himself for the 'fresh woods, and pastures new' of *Paradise Lost* ('Lycidas' 193).

Yet as I have already suggested, Milton's development is not that tidily teleological, nor was it predetermined or even foreknown. He was less sure of himself than we tend to assume in hindsight, and the course of events interrupted his plans. The process of writing itself changed his views and sent him off in new and perhaps unexpected directions: composing the elegies expected of a student poet made him confront loss and mortality, while working through *Comus* helped him rethink his idea of heaven and understanding of the place of sexuality in the good life. Thinking in poetry changed the way he thought.

Moreover, by the time Milton was able to write *Paradise Lost*, the epic was beginning to seem to many an outmoded genre, partly because of its association with classical myths. Relying on pagan gods, it appeared a throwback to a primitive world of superstition, a form inappropriate to a society enlightened both by Christianity and emerging science. Like many of the generation that had lived through Civil War—and like many today also who have come after the two world wars and Vietnam—Milton was also ambivalent about a genre that seemed too often to justify and even glorify mass slaughter.[1]

---

[1] Epics have always been more critical of heroic valour than we tend to suppose, however: both Homer and Virgil include critiques of war, presenting heroes who are themselves ambiguous role models, especially the sulkily angry Achilles and the wily and quite selfish Odysseus, who fights reluctantly and whose ultimate goal is to get

In both *Paradise Lost* and, as we will see later, *Paradise Regained*, he turns from 'Wars, hitherto the only argument / Heroic deemed' to celebrate alternative forms of action: 'the better fortitude / Of patience and heroic martyrdom / Unsung' (9.28–9, 31–2). When Milton first published *Paradise Lost*, in 1667, the title page did not identify it as an epic, but simply 'A Poem'. His first readers may have indeed expected a very different kind of poem, and wondered what kind of poem a regicide would write.

In fact, when Milton spoke of his future poetic plans in his prose writings of the 1640s and 1650s, he indicated that he was not certain what form his magnum opus would take nor what his subject would be. When he first started thinking about writing something like *Paradise Lost*, he imagined it not as an epic at all but as a tragedy. As *Comus* shows, he had a love of and flair for drama, the most exciting new literary form of his time. In the late sixteenth century, the English theatre had suddenly exploded as a new creative space, rapidly reaching a brilliant peak in the works of Shakespeare, which Milton studied carefully.[2] Drama, not old-fashioned epic, might well have seemed the form of the future. While as we saw in Chapter 1, some Protestant contemporaries were suspicious of the dubious moral influence of theatre, Milton went to plays, and in his early notebook or Commonplace book asserted 'For what in all philosophy is more serious or more sacred or more exalted than a tragedy rightly designed?'[3] In the 1640s, he sketched out some ideas for tragedies on the subject of '*Adam Unparadised*'. Milton's nephew, Edward Phillips, said that when he returned to this subject a bit later he was still thinking of it as

---

home to his wife and family. While writers believe that war is an inevitable part of human life, they also are aware of its damaging psychological and social effect, which is the subject of some of the greatest Greek tragedies.

[2] Critics have always intuited a relation between the two authors, noting especially echoes of Shakespeare's writing in the 1645 *Poems* and the similarity between Satan and Shakespearean villain-heroes like Richard III and Macbeth. Milton's first published poem was 'On Shakespeare', published in 1632 at the front of the Second Folio of Shakespeare's plays along with other tributes. A recent re-examination of a copy of Shakespeare's First Folio in the Free Library of Philadelphia has identified the marginalia as written in Milton's handwriting, offering us proof of Milton's familiarity and serious engagement with the plays.

[3] Cited from the *The Complete Works of John Milton*, Vol.11, ed. William Poole (Oxford: Oxford University Press, 2020), 278.

a play. According to Phillips, the first thing Milton wrote was the opening to Satan's address to the sun in *Paradise Lost* 4.32–41, a gloriously dramatic soliloquy, equal in psychological complexity to anything in Shakespeare. While at some point this drama turned into an epic, *Paradise Lost* as we have it is an unusually dramatic epic, with rich, living characters who debate and argue with each other and with themselves.

Unsure of what *kind* of major poem he would write, the young Milton also did not know what the *subject* of his great work would be. In his early notes, he jotted down possible topics, stories from the Bible and from British and Scottish history. He considered writing about King Arthur, England's great national hero and thus an obvious candidate for an English epic. In his notebook, however, Milton returned most often to the subject of the fall. In its scope, substance, and seriousness, the story in Genesis seems well-suited for an epic. Because Virgil had told the story of the founding of Rome, a Renaissance epic was often expected to narrate the origins of a nation. Genesis goes even further, telling the origins of the entire world, the beginnings not of *a* people but *all* people. It is an aetiological myth explaining why the world is the way it is; for a Christian of Milton's time, it was the most universal story of all.

To take on this story meant wrestling, however, with fundamental religious and philosophical questions concerning the nature of good and evil. As a creation myth, Genesis not only explains the origins of the entire cosmos, but tries to account for the existence of evil in this world. A key problem for a monotheistic religion is the difficulty of imagining a God who is both good and omnipotent. If God is omnipotent, he surely must have created evil, and so cannot be good; if he is good, he surely would not have created evil, and so cannot be omnipotent. Manicheans therefore claimed that the universe was divided between equally powerful forces of good and evil. The myth told in Genesis tries to resolve this problem. Its God is good and makes a good world in which he places his perfect creations, Adam and Eve. They themselves bring evil into the world by breaking a divine prohibition and eating from a forbidden tree of knowledge. But this leaves many other questions. If Eden is a perfect world, why does it include forbidden fruit? Why is eating from the tree specifically evil, and why is *knowledge* evil? Moreover, an omnipotent God knows everything and so would have foreknown the fall. Does this not then mean that he caused it after all, so that Adam and Eve never really had free will and are not responsible for their actions? And if Adam and Eve were created perfect, how could they do something wrong? In Genesis, the figure of the serpent who tricks Eve answers the last of these questions. But this in turn generates further problems: what is a talking serpent doing in the garden, and how could a serpent, or indeed any of God's creatures, be evil? The eventual identification by biblical scholars of the serpent with Satan, a fallen angel who becomes the devil and embodiment of evil, still comes back to the fundamental question: how could a good God make *anything* that would do something evil? How can good create evil without having been evil all along?

Some theologians, following St Augustine, accepted that such questions were a mystery that mortals shouldn't try to understand. Milton is less timid. As I noted, in his notebooks he seems repeatedly drawn to the story. From early on, it helps him understand his own experiences in life: in 'Lycidas', a young man's grappling with the consciousness of mortality brings about a kind of fall from a pastoral garden into a desert. Like most Christians of this time, Milton saw biblical stories as past history but also as narratives about his own life through which he could understand his experiences. The fall was something that had actually occurred at the beginning of time, but was also experienced by each individual in their own lives. The story of the transformation of a good world into a bad one may have seemed especially relevant after the Restoration, when, in Milton's view, the English perversely refused the chance to recover paradise on earth. The idea of the fall helps explain why instead of realizing a brave new world of human liberty they chose to return to a comfortable and familiar system of servitude. One does not have to believe in it to see that it is still a deeply resonant myth today, one that both explains why the world is as it is, but also tells us that it might be better.

Milton also shared the common belief that the Bible was the word of God through which the divine Creator spoke to his creatures. Like other Protestants, he assumed that Christians should read and interpret the Bible for themselves in order to know God, and indeed understand and make sense of themselves and the world around them. He spent many years working on a theological prose treatise, *On Christian Doctrine*, in which he offered his own interpretation of many of the central beliefs of Christianity. What Milton says there can be at times illuminating for reading his poetry. Still, *Paradise Lost* is a poem and not a theological treatise, and it draws on the power of poetry to try to understand these beliefs as well as Milton's own life. Its fundamental premise is that poetry, with its ability to sustain and dwell in paradoxes, to go in two (or more) directions at once, is the best means of approaching and understanding the problems generated by the story of Genesis, of reconciling the goodness of God with a world that is clearly not very good. Poetry can make the spiritual concrete because it can say different, even contradictory, things at once. It might therefore even be able to 'justify the ways of God to men' (*Paradise Lost* 1.26). In *Paradise Lost*, poetry and wordplay offer forms of creative knowledge that counter the destructive knowledge involved in the fall itself. Poetry helps us know God, the world, others, and ourselves.

Be Fruitful and Multiply: Elaborating Genesis

> And God blessed them, and God said unto them, Be fruitful, and multiply.
>
> Genesis 1:28

Never shy of tackling the impossible, Milton may well have been attracted to the story of Genesis precisely *because* it offered him so many challenges. It allows him to confront universal questions that are as pressing today as they were for him. The story poses artistic as well as religious problems. As a subject for a play, the story of Genesis would have been particularly difficult. In the drafts, Milton struggled to imagine how he might represent the unfallen Adam and Eve on stage. It is not just the issue of nudity: Milton seems equally concerned with the difficulty of imagining and presenting characters who are in a state of perfection. How can imperfect spectators relate to such figures—let alone to a transcendent, all-powerful God? An early draft opens with the character of Moses who tells the audience what is happening, explaining that 'they cannot see Adam in the state of innocence by reason of ... their sin'.[4] Allegorical figures representing

---

[4] Cited from *Paradise Lost*, ed. Barbara Kiefer Lewalski (Malden, MA: Blackwell, 2007), 342, though slightly modernized.

Justice and Mercy then come on stage to debate what will happen after the fall.

This is not a promising start. It looks surprisingly undramatic, old-fashioned, and downright dull. Static and too talky, it is more like a medieval morality play than anything written by Shakespeare or the playwrights of Milton's own time. The narrative form of epic freed Milton's imagination from the demands of staging, allowing him to represent dynamic and sweeping cosmic action, including an epic war in heaven. Moving beyond the flat, allegorical, figures of the early drafts, he was able to create complex and truly dramatic characters, and to present the fall through distinct and sometimes conflicting points of view and perspectives.

A second problem with Milton's choice of subject was noted by Dr. Johnson, who complained that the story told in *Paradise Lost* is too familiar to Christian readers steeped in the Genesis tradition.[5] How can there be any suspense when, from the very start, readers know that Adam and Eve will fall? This is both a poetic and religious problem, related to the vexed question of the free will or agency of the hero. In classical epics, the hero is doomed to a foreknown fate that he cannot resist. Milton highlights this question early on. The first thing that God does when he appears in *Paradise Lost* 3 is remind us of the end of the story: Adam and Eve will fall. The end seems predetermined from the very start, so that Adam and Eve have no free will. Even worse, the plot seems a trap set for Eve in particular. Modern readers of Milton, even students who are not Christians and barely know the story, have heard enough to suspect that the Genesis story is generally part of a patriarchal plot to keep women down. Historically it certainly has been used that way. But Milton strongly believes that Adam and Eve had free will and were able to make real choices.[6] He does not want a deity who programmes the couple to fall and then punishes them for doing so. He also believes passionately that human actions have meaning and importance. As he retells Genesis, therefore, Milton tries to free it and us from our preconceptions about the story

---

[5] See the 'Life of Milton', 107.

[6] In his theological treatise on *Christian Doctrine*, Milton states: 'The matter or object of the divine plan was that angels and men alike should be endowed with free will' (Kerrigan, 1157). In *Paradise Lost* even Satan privately admits this, when he speaks to himself: 'Hadst thou the same free will and power to stand? / Thou hadst: whom hast thou then or what to accuse, / But Heav'n's free love dealt equally to all?' (4.66–8).

and its meaning. He asks his readers to think in new ways about questions they may have felt closed, to grapple with the significance of the problems raised not only by the Bible but by the interpretive tradition that over centuries had arisen around it. Despite the reader's as well as God's foreknowledge, Milton wants to create suspense by making us believe that the actions could have had another outcome.

It's a difficult task, but poetry offers him ways of achieving it. The story told in Genesis is very short. The Bible tells us what happens in the simplest and plainest way possible: the world is made, Adam and Eve are created, a snake suddenly appears and speaks to Eve, Eve and Adam eat the fruit, God kicks them out of the garden. This stark narrative gives us no explanation of the causes or motives of the actions, or even the relations between them. Things just happen. The most obvious and in some ways important difference between Genesis and *Paradise Lost* is that of length, as Milton fills in the gaps in this skeletal story. In Genesis the fall takes place in six short verses. The climactic moment of transgression takes place in a single sentence in which Adam's fall is barely distinct from that of Eve: 'And when the woman saw that the tree *was* good for food, and that it *was* pleasant to the eyes, and a tree to be desired to make *one* wise, she took of the fruit thereof, and did eat, and gave also unto her husband with her; and he did eat' (Genesis 3:6).

In contrast, Milton's account in Book 9 stretches out to almost 1,200 lines of verse and separates the two falls. As we'll see further, where Genesis presents only the basic action, Milton fills in the context and shows a couple deliberating and debating before they act, and making difficult and life-changing individual choices. In Genesis, moreover, the unfolding of events is relentlessly linear: we begin with the beginning of everything (the creation of the world!) and move forward through a chain of events that leads to the fall and then from there directly to the rest of the history told in the Bible that climaxes with the end of the world in the Book of Revelation. As the image of the chain suggests, such a presentation makes the actions seem a closely linked sequence of causes and effects which follow one from another inevitably and in which Adam and Eve are helplessly bound. Instead of telling the story in this chronological way—which in general of course could be rather dull and plodding—Milton, copying Homer and Virgil, begins in medias res, in the middle of things, after the fall of Satan from heaven. The actual beginning, the story of Satan's fall from heaven and the creation of the world, is put in the middle of the epic (Books 5–8). The poem thus moves in two directions at once: both forwards in time towards the fall of Adam and Eve and backwards through flashbacks to the fall of Satan. This elaboration and disruption of linear time, with which Milton had experimented in the 'Nativity Ode', suggests further that the chain of events might have been broken. Milton slows down and complicates the actions to build suspense. Despite his own and our foreknowledge, he pushes us to imagine that the story might have gone in a different direction as Adam and Eve really *could* have made other choices.

Answerable Style

Milton thus uses the structure of the poem to open up possibilities and create dramatic suspense. The poetic form he chose is also crucial to this goal: blank verse, unrhymed iambic pentameter feet (five short/long feet). This was a surprising choice for Milton, especially in 1667. Renaissance epics were most often written in rhyme: in the sixteenth century, the ottava rima (an eight-line stanza organized ABABABCC) that ends 'Lycidas', and, towards the end of the seventeenth century, heroic couplets (AABBCC etc.).[7] As we saw, the young Milton used

---

[7] John Harington's 1591 published translation of the Italian Ariosto's *Orlando Furioso* is, like the original, written in ottava rima. This is the opening:

Of DAMES, of knights, of arms, of love's delight,	A
Of courtesies, of high attempts I speak,	B
Then when the Moors transported all their might	A
On Afric seas, the force of France to break:	B
Incited by the youthful heat and spite	A
Of Agramant their king, that vowed to wreak	B
The death of King Trayano, lately slain,	C
Upon the Roman Emperour Charlemagne.	C

(1.1–8)

Cited from *Ariosto's Orlando Furioso. Selections from the Translation of Sir John Harington*, ed. Rudolf Gottfried (Bloomington and London: Indiana University Press, 1971).

Milton's contemporary Abraham Cowley used the more expected rhyming couplets for his epic based on the biblical story of David, *Davideis* (1656), which opens:

I sing the man who Judah's scepter bore	A
In that right hand which held the crook before;	A
Who from best poet, best of kings did grow;	B
The two chief gifts heaven could on Man bestow.	B

rhyming patterns skilfully and meaningfully in his earlier works. He is attentive to the power of poetic forms to incarnate his themes and seems to find the limitations of form liberating and empowering. They challenge him creatively: throughout his life he wrote sonnets, one of the most intricate and restrictive poetic forms, and his last major poem, *Samson Agonistes*, uses rhyme freely though erratically. Yet in the preface to the 1668 edition of *Paradise Lost* he attacks rhyme as 'no necessary adjunct or true ornament of poem or good verse, in longer works especially, but the invention of a barbarous age, to set off wretched matter and lame meter', and offers his unrhymed verse as 'an example set, the first in English, of ancient liberty recovered to heroic poem from the troublesome and modern bondage of rhyming' (Kerrigan, 291). He presents himself as a poetical revolutionary, heroically freeing language from inhibiting and unnatural customs.[8] For later writers, especially those in the twentieth century, Milton seems the ancestor of what we tellingly call 'free verse'.

Yet the form Milton has chosen is hardly like modern free verse—in comparison to twentieth- to twenty-first-century poetry it seems extremely formal, staid, even monolithic and monumental. Visually it creates walls of equal and imposing lines arranged in dense and often lengthy verse paragraphs (look at the example below to see what I mean). The form deliberately calls attention to its difference from mere prose, especially as Milton's often Latinate-sounding language and strange word order can appear formal and sometimes unnatural. But solid as Milton's form may appear to a modern reader, it is remarkably dynamic and flexible. Blank verse balances freedom and order. Structured by its breakdown into lines of five iambic feet but unfettered by the requirements of rhyme, it can propel narrative and

Much danger first, much toil did he sustain,   C
Whilst Saul and Hell crossed his strong fate in vain.   C

Taken from *Abraham Cowley: Poems; Miscellanies, The Mistress, Pindarique Odes, Davideis, Verses Written on Several Occasions*, ed. A. R. Waller (Cambridge: Cambridge University Press, 1905), p. 242, lines 1–6. I have modernized Cowley's spelling.

[8] The significance of rhyme had of course changed since Milton's youth; he seems to be responding in particular to the Restoration dominance of heroic couplets, a form which can create an appearance of harmony and the resolution of differences. In contrast, Milton's verse, even when rhymed, often resists too reassuring or complete closure.

thought forward to express complex ideas. Although the lines are all equal in length, the absence of rhyming words to mark the end of lines enables the verse to be fluid and expansive. Milton's lines are also often enjambed, so that they run on without pause to form longer verse paragraphs. The famous opening of *Paradise Lost* sweeps up the first sixteen lines into a single sentence:

> Of man's first disobedience, and the fruit
> Of that forbidden tree, whose mortal taste
> Brought death into the world, and all our woe,
> With loss of Eden, till one greater man
> Restore us, and regain the blissful seat,
> Sing heav'nly Muse, that on the secret top
> Of Oreb, or of Sinai, didst inspire
> That shepherd, who first taught the chosen seed,
> In the beginning how the heavens and earth
> Rose out of Chaos: or if Sion hill
> Delight thee more, and Siloa's brook that flowed
> Fast by the oracle of God, I thence
> Invoke thy aid to my advent'rous song,
> That with no middle flight intends to soar
> Above th' Aonian mount, while it pursues
> Things unattempted yet in prose or rhyme.   (1.1–16)

This is a demanding passage to read and especially to read aloud, because with the lack of rhymes or marked pauses at the end of lines it's hard to find a place to breathe. The suspension of verbs—the main verb, 'Sing', here doesn't come in till the sixth line—is not only unnatural and confusing but keeps us rushing forward to get to the action.[9] It's as if once the poet starts to speak he can't stop until he is soaring above the ancient poets, associated with the Aonian Mount, home of the classical Muses, in order to do something completely original. The opening shows the eagerness to get ahead that we saw in the 'Nativity Ode', perhaps increased after years away from poetry. Finally getting his chance at the big time, the narrator is bursting with

---

[9] Critics often observe that Milton's training in writing in Latin, a language which often postpones the verb for effect, influenced his thinking in English. As we saw earlier, he doesn't like us to get to the meaning too quickly and often makes us wait to get the complete idea.

energy and wants to talk about everything at once: in the first five lines alone, Milton jumps from the beginning of history told in the Bible ('man's first disobedience', 1) to the coming of Christ ('one greater man', 4), from the story of the fall to that of redemption, from the beginning of the Bible to its end. As in the 'Nativity Ode', he wants to transcend time. Where rhyme might hold him back, as it did in the 'Nativity Ode', here the language and thought seem to push forward freely without restraint. Rhyme is predictable: it gives the reader a sense of where the verse might be going ('June' always seems inevitably to lead to 'tune' or 'honeymoon'). It works against suspense, as meaning seems predetermined by sound, and so is not appropriate for what Milton is trying to do here. Instead, the language and thought of *Paradise Lost* seem able to go anywhere. To make it even harder to predict where the poem is heading, words change meaning before our eyes. The word 'fruit' has one meaning in line one and another in line two: in the first line it is used figuratively, to mean the consequence or result of disobedience, but in the second line it suddenly becomes also the literal fruit of the tree that caused the disobedience. The lines don't ask us to choose between the two meanings, however, but create a complex identification between them. In the first two lines, Milton plunges us into an expansive way of thinking and knowing, demanding that we be ready to follow him anywhere. While we know already how the story ends, the fact that we can't tell where or how a sentence will finish creates suspense and pushes back against the feeling of inevitability. With its formal language and often unnatural arrangement of syntax the poem makes us think differently, asking us to imagine new possibilities and, especially, a world that might be other than it is.

Blank verse further helps Milton present a new perspective on a familiar story through the creation of character and different points of view. As I noted earlier, most epics of this time were written in rhyme. Blank verse was associated primarily with drama. Its dramatic power had first been realized by Marlowe, though it was Shakespeare of course who made it the ideal form for describing the mind in motion. It is especially good for showing characters who are working out decisions and choices through dramatic soliloquy. Hamlet could never have decided 'To be or not to be' in rhyme: the need to find rhyming words would have overdetermined the outcome and so

hampered the decision-making process.[10] As we saw in the last chapter,
Milton had tried out blank verse earlier in *Comus*, using it primarily for
the good characters to express the rational choices they make, and
contrasting it with Comus's appealing but dangerous sing-song rhymes
in which sound can drown sense.

In *Paradise Lost*, blank verse allows Milton to harness the power of
drama and dramatic suspense for an epic so that we see old stories
from different perspectives: not only that of the narrator but also
of God himself, the Son, Adam, Eve, Satan, and some of the good
angels. It brings to life characters who could easily become, as in his
early drafts, rather flat allegorical figures or archetypes. As in the theatre, direct speech makes us feel as if we see into the minds of the
speaker. So while Satan is introduced as 'the author of all ill' (2.381),
from the very beginning he is a complex dramatic figure whose language seductively draws us into his way of thinking. We first meet him
after he has been driven down to hell, where he gloomily assesses his
situation. He addresses his first speech to his sidekick, Beelzebub, who
seems as changed as their circumstances:

> If thou beest he; but O how fall'n! How changed
> From him, who in the happy realms of light
> Clothed with transcendent brightness didst outshine
> Myriads though bright: if he whom mutual league,
> United thoughts and counsels, equal hope

[10] A more instructive comparison might be the deliberation of Satan in rhymed
couplets in John Dryden's 1674 rhymed and dramatic version of *Paradise Lost, The State
of Innocence*. Scrapping the narrator completely, it opens with the newly fallen Satan
speaking in hell:

> Is this the Seat our Conquerour has given?
> And this the Climate we must change for Heaven?
> These Regions and these Realms my Wars have got:
> This mournful Empire is the loser's Lot:
> In liquid Burnings, or on dry to dwell,
> Is all the sad variety of Hell.

From *The State of Innocence, and Fall of Man: An Opera* (London: Printed for Hen.
Herringman, 1695), lines 1–6.

The rhymes and the rhyming couplets contribute to an emphasis on balance and
symmetry that limits what Satan can say or think; all the wide variety of Milton's vision
is reduced to either/or oppositions: Climate (of hell) or heaven; liquid or dry. John
Creaser has written a series of wonderful essays on Milton's style, using this contrast
with Dryden; see the suggestions for 'Further Reading' at the end of the book.

> And hazard in the glorious enterprise,
> Joined with me once, now misery hath joined
> In equal ruin: into what pit thou seest
> From what highth fall'n, so much the stronger proved
> He with his thunder: and till then who knew
> The force of those dire arms?   (1.84–94)

While the verse form is the same as in the opening lines of the poem, the movement here is strikingly different. Milton shows how he can use one form for very different effects. Where the narrator sweeps everything into a single breathless sixteen-line sentence, Satan has difficulty formulating a complete coherent sentence and breaks off his first thought after four words with a 'but': 'If thou beest he; *but* O'. The twisting and choppy syntax throughout these lines suggests his disorientation in a new world in which he can barely recognize his best friend or even himself as both are 'how fall'n! How changed' (84). In his fall, he has fallen apart, as his bewildered mind is trapped in circles, spinning around memories of the past and a sense of loss, disorientation, and sheer horror at his present situation.

But there is something compellingly driven about this tortuous mind and, as Satan continues to speak, he starts to pull himself together:

> Yet not for those,
> Nor what the potent victor in his rage
> Can else inflict, do I repent or change,
> Though changed in outward luster; that fixed mind
> And high disdain, from sense of injured merit,
> That with the mightiest raised me to contend,
> And to the fierce contention brought along
> Innumerable force of spirits armed
> That durst dislike his reign, and me preferring,
> His utmost power with adverse power opposed
> In dubious battle on the plains of Heav'n,
> And shook his throne.   (1.94–105)

A master plotter from the start, Satan takes control of the narrative. Remembering the fight against God, he begins to build an image of himself as a courageous leader who challenged an evil oppressor. In his version of the story of the fall, God is a tempter and tyrant and he himself is the hero not the villain. Over the centuries he has convinced many readers to agree with him, beginning with William Blake. But the movement of the language lets us watch this self-creation unfold: with sinuous syntax appropriate for a future snake, he moves from hesitation and uncertainty ('If ... if'; 84, 87), building to a grand climax in which he asserts a firmly determined and immutable purpose in almost monumental phrasing:

> What though the field be lost?
> All is not lost; the unconquerable will,
> And study of revenge, immortal hate,
> And courage never to submit or yield:
> And what is else not to be overcome?   (1.105–9)

The sheer force of Satan's 'unconquerable will' is so impressive that it is easy to focus on his own proclaimed 'courage' and determination, and overlook some of the shadier implications in his speech, such as the fact that he is driven by 'revenge' and 'hate'. Starting as someone whose language and identity seem to be breaking down, he quickly gathers himself together to become the master of the memorable and powerful short phrase—which is why so many of his lines are often quoted. We see a paradoxical transformation as Satan grapples with radical change to ultimately deny change altogether: he will not 'repent or change, / Though changed in outward luster' (1.96–7).[11] Though his circumstances and appearances are quite different, he proclaims proudly that he is still the same inside; so he claims that he is:

> one who brings
> A mind not to be changed by place or time.
> The mind is its own place, and in itself
> Can make a Heav'n of Hell, a Hell of Heav'n.
> What matter where, if I be still the same.   (1.252–6)

I'll return to Satan's defiant insistence on personal consistency and autonomy later. But Milton's decision to begin the poem with a devil's-eye view of the story is daring and exciting. He makes us know

---

[11] Satan's speedy character development from uncertainty to infernal stability is mirrored in the devils' movement through space in Book 1: beginning on a lake of burning fire, the fallen angels march to more comfortable and secure dry land on which they can walk and then build themselves and Satan a splendidly solid palace.

how evil *thinks*, thrusting us immediately into Satan's mind and getting us on his side. Satan's determination, his refusal to give in and insistence on the power of the mind to remake its world, can seem heroic and compelling, especially as it recalls the stubbornly loyal Milton who would not give up hope in the English revolution even when it was collapsing. Milton makes us confront the attraction and easy familiarity of evil. We use the terms good and evil as if they conveyed perfectly obvious and antithetical moral absolutes that everyone can recognize. For Milton, however, the fall itself makes it difficult to differentiate the two; as he explained in *Areopagitica*: 'Good and evil we know in the field of this world grow up together almost inseparably; and the knowledge of good is so involved and interwoven with the knowledge of evil, and in so many cunning resemblances hardly to be discerned' (Kerrigan, 938). But books themselves can help us disentangle the two, as they allow us to see and know evil without actually doing it: 'bad books, . . . to a discreet and judicious reader serve in many respects to discover, to confute, to forewarn, and to illustrate' (Kerrigan, 938). In *Paradise Lost*, the difficulty of distinguishing good and evil will prove a problem for Adam and Eve, and also for the reader and author himself. It is poetry itself, however, that makes all the difference.

Making Makers

If it is easy for us to identify with the heroic and dramatic Satan, it is nearly impossible for us to do so with Milton's God. Presenting him on stage would have been unimaginable, and even in a narrative form it is very difficult to represent the transcendent creator of the world. Many readers have found Milton's God unattractive, or at least an unsuccessful depiction of a good God.[12] He can seem rigid and dogmatic, and I doubt many, if any, readers would nominate him for the role of the poem's hero. We get to see the story from his point of view in Book 3 when we move to heaven, where, as I noted earlier, God himself takes on the central problem of accountability for the fall. Where Satan, like us, sees only in bits and pieces, the omniscient God

[12] Most famously, the modern critic William Empson wrote a provocative attack on Milton's God, one which in many ways is really an attack on Christianity as a whole; see his still stimulating *Milton's God* (London: Chatto & Windus, 1961).

can take everything in at once. His syntax thus unfolds more smoothly and straightforwardly, but lacks the interest of Satan's twisting thought. Announcing that the fall will happen, he still insists that Adam's and Eve's choice is made of their own free will:

> they themselves decreed
> Their own revolt, not I: if I foreknew,
> Foreknowledge had no influence on their fault,
> Which had no less proved certain unforeknown.
> So without least impulse or shadow of fate,
> Or aught by me immutably foreseen,
> They trespass, authors to themselves in all
> Both what they judge and what they choose; for so
> I formed them free, and free they must remain,
> Till they enthrall themselves.   (3.116–25)

Milton directly confronts the theological paradox of the relation between human free will and divine foreknowledge by making God himself say that the latter does not impinge upon the former. Though God *knows* what will happen, he does not *make* it happen, and Adam and Eve are free to choose their own damnation.

Having God present this key point of doctrine gives it an authoritative ring. After all, he should know. Yet the speech can seem rather defensive, self-justifying, and even somewhat peevish. Milton's God can also appear rather egocentric; while he attributes the fall to Adam's and Eve's freely made choice, he insists that their redemption will occur only because of *his* divine grace and generosity. After the fall, human actions are meaningless, as he explains:

> Man shall not quite be lost, but saved who will,
> Yet not of will in him, but grace in *me*
> Freely vouchsafed;...
>   ...that he may know how frail
> His fall'n condition is, and to *me* owe
> All his deliv'rance, and to none but *me*.   (3.173–5, 180–2; emphasis added)

This is a conventional Protestant belief of course, and it is hard to imagine a God who would not seem almost narcissistically self-centred, given that he is traditionally both centre and circumference of the universe. A transcendent deity is by definition unknowable, beyond the reach of human comprehension and certainly modern expectations of 'relatability'.

If God the Father is remote and unknowable, however, the Son, who will come down to earth and unite the divine with the human, is a God we can know. In Book 3, as we move to heaven, Milton reminds us that the Son is 'The radiant image' of the Father (3.63) who allows us to glimpse the ineffable:

> Begotten Son, divine similitude,
> In whose conspicuous count'nance, without cloud
> Made visible, th' Almighty Father shines,
> Whom else no creature can behold.   (3.384–7)

The Son expresses aspects of God that are otherwise hidden from us. Here, he seems to show God's best features: offering to sacrifice himself for mankind, the Son radiates 'Divine compassion', 'Love without end, and without measure grace' (3.141, 142). As we saw in reading the 'Nativity Ode', moreover, Milton sees the Son as embodying the creativity that is essential to his concept of the divine. In Book 7 especially, the Son makes accessible God's essential power as the 'Maker omnipotent' (4.725), 'The great Creator' (7.567), by creating the world.

Milton's lengthy and exuberant elaboration of the creation of the world in Genesis puts the Son and the act of creation itself at the heart of his poem. He gives us a great deal more detail about the process than is in the Bible, focusing on *how* the Son creates as well as *what* he creates. Breaking away from the orthodox beliefs of the time, Milton does not believe that the world was made from nothing, but out of chaos. For him, all creation is recreation, especially his own. The poet's creation of *Paradise Lost* out of the materials of tradition—not only the Bible but classical mythology and epic, as well as earlier European and English writings—is itself an extension of the Son's ordering of chaos. Before creation, chaos is a 'vast immeasurable abyss / Outrageous as a sea, dark, wasteful, wild' (7.211–12), in which waves surge 'as mountains to assault / Heav'n's highth, and with the center mix the pole' (7.214–15). Like an artist outlining a painting or architect designing the foundations of a building, the Son draws out 'golden compasses' (7.225), and gives the world a new shape by drawing boundaries around this unruly space.

Many creation myths of other cultures imagine the god who makes the world as a creator. But Milton's portrayal of divine creativity is highly unusual. In the Judaeo-Christian tradition, the creating God is male, a version of an archetypal sky father figure who constructs a world without a female partner. This kind of myth is often contrasted with one found in other religions in which the world is born out of an earth mother. While Milton's Father and Son are at least nominally male, the divine seems to expand to include both male and female principles. The Son both impregnates and broods over chaos, when: 'on the wat'ry calm / His brooding wings the Spirit of God outspread, / And vital virtue infused' (7.234–6). The act of divine creativity seems beyond distinctions of gender. Moreover, the Son is presented not only as an artist or architect working on his materials but also as a lover embracing and mingling his nature with theirs. For Milton, creativity is not a disembodied intellectual experience but one that involves both body and mind. As I noted earlier, the association of the imagination with the erotic has made many thinkers attack poetry as dangerously arousing. Yet this ability to move us is what makes it powerful and completely human. Milton imagines creativity as a kind of intercourse that involves an intimate and loving relation between creator and the creation into which he pours himself.[13]

Because of that, divine creativity also disrupts the distinction between creator and created. Milton's God generates creativity in others, beginning in Book 7 when the newly created earth then gives birth to new beings (a scene that itself enables Milton to infuse Genesis's patriarchal narrative with elements from alternative matriarchal mythologies). In classical mythology especially, deities envy and punish mortals who show imagination and initiative. Prometheus is tortured for bringing fire to mankind—an act seen as the origin of all other human inventions. Ovid's enormously influential collection of myths in the *Metamorphoses* presents a series of mortals who challenge the artistry of the gods and in consequence meet nasty ends: the weaver Arachne who claims to surpass Minerva in skill is turned into a spider for her uppityness; the satyr Marsyas who challenges Apollo to a singing match is flayed alive (a scene which has especially fascinated later artists). Classical gods want to keep the power of

[13] Milton is not often compared to John Donne, whose poems blurred the sexual and the sacred, using erotic imagery to describe Donne's relation with God and religious imagery to imagine his relation to his lovers. But like Donne, the major influence on writers of Milton's generation, Milton wants us to think seriously about the deep bond between the carnal and the spiritual or intellectual.

creation for themselves alone as a means of reinforcing the difference
between humans and mortals. But Milton's God has a less dualistic
and absolute sense of the relation of the divine to the human; as the
idea of the incarnation itself indicates, the boundary he draws
between the human and the divine is permeable. For Milton, the God
who makes man in his own image makes more makers, beginning
with the Son himself, his firstborn. This act in turn inspires others to
create. God's creativity spurs the angels to burst out into spontaneous
song themselves: seeing the Son's work, they rejoice:

> with joy and shout
> The hollow universal orb they filled,
> And touched their golden harps, and hymning praised
> God and his works; Creator him they sung,
> Both when first ev'ning was, and when first morn. (7.256–60)

God's creation becomes the source of and subject for creation in
others; it inspires in turn the narrator himself who invokes as his Muse
the Holy Ghost who 'with mighty wings outspread / Dove-like sat'st
brooding on the vast abyss / And mad'st it pregnant' (1.20–2). The
divine power of creativity, here again imagined as erotic intercourse
that fuses female and male roles, is at the centre of the universe as well
as Milton's poem, radiating out and informing all created life, and
identifying the creator with his creatures.

The First Garden of Verses

Milton's Eden is alive with creative energy. As I noted in the preface,
it is not a formally arranged garden with carefully clipped trees but a
place of luxury and abundance:

> A wilderness of sweets; for nature here
> Wantoned as in her prime, and played at will
> Her virgin fancies, pouring forth more sweet,
> Wild above rule or art; enormous bliss. (5.294–7)

Nature pours forth itself 'above rule or art'; it is 'grotesque and wild'
(4.136), and its 'rich trees wept odorous gums and balm' (4.248). As
Milton and any gardener knows, however, nature runs the danger of

being choked by its own fertility: plants need cutting back.[14] Adam and Eve's task in the garden is therefore to prune it so that, paradoxically, it 'grows, / Luxurious by restraint' (9.208–9). Like the Son who creates by shaping chaos and giving it limits—telling it 'thus far thy bounds' (7.230)—Adam and Eve prune the plants to create and define their world and, at the same time, themselves.

The fact that Milton's first couple work at all, however, is itself remarkable. We tend to think of work and recreation as antitheses (though this antithesis seems challenged today when sometimes it is hard to mark any boundaries between the two, and work threatens to swallow our last scraps of privacy). Given the negative associations of work, many other representations of the golden age or biblical Eden imagined it as a kind of leisure garden and labour as a punishment for human transgression (see not only the story told in Genesis 3 but also classical works such as Hesiod's *Works and Days* and Virgil's *Georgics*). For Milton, however, prelapsarian work is a form of pleasurable and creative play, as tending the garden is itself a means by which Adam and Eve show their likeness to their maker. Through looking after the garden, Adam and Eve actively participate in making their own world and so both repeat and extend God's originary act. They are not passive recipients of God's bounty who simply dwell in the space handed to them, but shapers of the world they live in. God may make the garden, but it is the daily work of Adam and Eve that keeps it as a paradise. Milton builds also on an ancient tradition in which gardening, as the transformation of nature through human intervention, is used as a symbol for art generally and poetry in particular.[15] Perhaps because of

---

[14] See the description of Adam and Eve's labour in 5.211–19:

> On to their morning's rural work they haste
> Among sweet dews and flow'rs; where any row
> Of fruit trees over-woody reached too far
> Their pampered boughs, and needed hands to check
> Fruitless embraces: or they led the vine
> To wed her elm; she spoused about him twines
> Her marriageable arms, and with her brings
> Her dow'r th' adopted clusters, to adorn
> His barren leaves.

Without their work even Eden's fertile world is 'fruitless' and 'barren'.

[15] The Latin verb 'to think', *putare*, also means 'to prune'. Milton is clearly also drawing on Virgil's *Georgics*, a poem on farming which sees the figures of the farmer, poet, and heroic leader as part of the same essential struggle to create order in the world.

the British love of gardens, British writers have always enjoyed playing with the pun that identifies posies (flowers) and poesy (poetry) that I noted earlier, as may be seen in works ranging from George Gascoigne's 1573 *A Hundred Sundrie Flowers* (revised as *The Posies of George Gascoigne*) to Robert Louis Stevenson's 1885 *A Child's Garden of Verses*.

Milton's paradise brings to life the old pun between gardening and poetry by rooting it in our original experience. But Milton's Adam and Eve are literally as well as figuratively poets who enjoy playing with words. Through creative language the couple show their likeness to the creator God and actively turn Eden into a garden of poetry as well as posies. Wordplay allows them to know themselves, each other, and the world around them. They speak to each other rather formally, even ceremoniously, as quite elaborate language comes naturally to them. When Adam first talks with Eve he doesn't call her simply by her name, 'Eve', but addresses her tenderly and playfully as the 'Sole partner and sole part of all these joys' (4.411). The lines wittily express both his love and his respect for her, as well as his delight in their relationship: she is his *sole* partner, the only creature in Eden who is his equal, but also his *soul* partner. If the pun on sole/soul is clever, however, the play on part/partner is even better. The simple word 'part' has many different meanings: a part can be a piece of something; as a verb it can mean to separate things or to share (partake of) something. Here it demonstrates the complex, dynamic, and creative relationship between husband and wife who, beginning as literally one flesh, were separated, but are now reunited as parts of a new whole in which they are only symbolically 'one flesh'. With rather astonishing skill for a newly created being, Adam compresses the couple's entire dating history into a single line. Eve began as a *part* of him but is now his *partner*; it is because he *parted* from her (he was in fact taken *apart*) that he is able to *part* (share) his life with her. Importantly, in Adam's address the relation between these different meanings is not one of conflict—we are not forced to choose one single meaning alone—but rather, and appropriately, one of complementarity and *partner*ship. The different senses are all joined, in fact, as *parts* of a single narrative sequence which tells the story of Eve's creation. The ability of words to mean many things at once is a source of enormous pleasure for the couple, as it is for Milton himself who often chooses words that seem to point in different directions that the speakers themselves may not foresee. Our own words open up new possibilities that can be beyond our control: that is the source of their great power, though also therefore, as we will see further, of their danger. Another common meaning of 'part' of course, is a role in a play or performance. This is the meaning Satan knows (see *Paradise Lost* 9.763); it suggests that, as we'll see later, parting and division and wordplay itself can also lead to alienation and deception.

As a means of communication, wordplay brings the couple together as distinct individuals and yet connected partners. But Milton's couple do not only talk in the garden. We first see them sharing a meal together, and the discussion with Raphael in Books 5–8 takes place over a tasty lunch. Bodily pleasure is central to Milton's vision of Eden. As many readers have noted, today generally with approval, Milton especially draws attention to and celebrates Adam's and Eve's lovemaking. While the sensuality of his Eden is one thing that might make it attractive to us, it is also unusual for its time. For many earlier Christian thinkers, sex, like work, was a result of the fall. In the tradition of the Virgilian epic too, erotic love always impedes heroic action and so must be set aside.[16] But sex is one of the purest pleasures and noblest pursuits Milton can imagine, and a central part of the ideal life. Physical pleasure is not superficial or superfluous but essential to the relationship between Adam and Eve, the means by which they know each other fully as embodied beings and show their love for each other. For Milton, conversation and sex are the two primary ways we may intimately know an other and express our love. Sexual intercourse complements and completes the verbal intercourse which is a source of intense and creative delight for both Adam and Eve, a means by which they express love and understand their relationship to each other.

In the passage above, Adam celebrates Eve as a part who is now, to his delight, a partner with whom he may come together verbally and sexually. Eve shares Adam's love of language, through which she can show her equal joy in their love. As part of their conversation that evening, Adam reminds Eve of their task and the rules of the garden.

---

[16] As Satan assumes in *Paradise Regained* when he dismisses contemptuously Belial's suggestion that the devils use women to tempt Jesus. He argues that the Son of God is above such low pleasures and they must try him with 'manlier objects' (*Paradise Regained* 2.225).

He praises their pleasant job and easy working conditions: 'our delightful task / To prune these growing plants, and tend these flow'rs, / Which were it toilsome, yet with thee were *sweet*' (4.437–9; emphasis added). Work is a means of experiencing the pleasure which is the goal of Milton's perfect life. As they then prepare to go to bed, Eve rather abruptly bursts into poetry. Glossing Adam's final word 'sweet', she elaborates his short description of their life so that it becomes a lyric on their world and their love:

> *Sweet* is the breath of morn, her rising *sweet*,
> With charm of earliest birds; pleasant the sun
> When first on this delightful land he spreads
> His orient beams, on herb, tree, fruit, and flow'r,
> Glist'ring with dew; fragrant the fertile earth
> After soft showers; and *sweet* the coming on
> Of grateful evening mild, then silent night
> With this her solemn bird and this fair moon,
> And these the gems of heav'n, her starry train:
> But neither breath of morn when she ascends
> With charm of earliest birds, nor rising sun
> On this delightful land, nor herb, fruit, flow'r,
> Glist'ring with dew, nor fragrance after showers,
> Nor grateful evening mild, nor silent night
> With this her solemn bird, nor walk by moon,
> Or glittering starlight without thee is *sweet*.   (4.641–56; emphasis added)

Like the luxurious garden which it celebrates, Eve's verbal abundance and ingenuity pours itself forth. At the same time, the artful and precise crafting of this spontaneous sixteen-line lyric outburst is quite stunning. Delicately and carefully shaped, it forms a beautifully unified and self-contained circle, beginning and ending with Adam's final word 'sweet'. The word also frames the opening line, '*Sweet* is the breath of morn, her rising *sweet*' (641), creating a small verbal circle within the larger structure and so reflecting an ordered universe of correspondences in which the microcosm mirrors the larger macrocosm. Like 'part', 'sweet' plays a key role in capturing the essence of life in the garden. Eden is full of 'odorous sweets' (4.166), 'A wilderness of sweets' (5.294) where nature 'played at will / Her virgin fancies, pouring forth more sweet' (5.295–6); while the bower in which Adam and Eve make love and sleep is specifically full of 'sweet-smelling herbs' (4.709). The couple enjoy their 'sweet gard'ning labor' (4.328) and 'sweet repast' (8.214, 9.407)—suggesting the likeness between earth and heaven where the angels also savour their 'sweet repast' and 'communion sweet' (5.630, 637). Eve's love lyric celebrates the sweetness of the natural world and the joy it gives her, following the cycles of the day from 'the breath of morn' to the coming of 'silent night'. In line 650, however, the poem reverses direction with the word 'But'. The last seven lines circle back to repeat the first but also negate them, explaining that while nature expresses sweetness it is not its source. As we saw earlier, Milton's words and lines can turn in unexpected ways, demanding that we pay careful attention. In Eve's lyric the celebration of the sweetness of nature swerves now into praise of *Adam*, who for her is the source of all the sweetness in the world.

She for God in Him

This is obviously highly flattering for Adam, as it makes him the centre of Eve's universe. It might confirm an impression of the relation between the couple created by Milton's first description of them in Book 4 in which we meet them after a day of work, as they enjoy dinner together surrounded by the animals of Eden.

Taking in the landscape of the dynamic Eden, Milton suddenly focuses in on the pair whose relation is at the very heart of his perfect world. After the description of the exuberant setting, this portrait seems rather static, as if the action abruptly stopped dead so that the characters could arrange themselves for a snapshot that captures their characters and relationship to each other. At first, things look quite promising, as they appear:

> Two of far nobler shape erect and tall,
> Godlike erect, with native honor clad
> In naked majesty seemed lords of all,
> And worthy seemed, for in their looks divine
> The image of their glorious Maker shone,
> Truth, wisdom, sanctitude severe and pure,
> Severe but in true filial freedom placed;
> Whence true authority in men.   (4.288–95)

So far so good: both Adam and Eve are 'lords of all', 'The image' of God, equipped with 'wisdom' and capable of 'true filial freedom'.

In fact, there seems no real difference between the two sexes at all. But suddenly, devastatingly, difference comes in, so that man and woman are divided firmly in terms of contrasting attributes and made part of a hierarchy, in which God is on top, Adam in the middle, and Eve (surprise!) at the bottom. The two may look just the same but, we are told grimly, they are:

> Not equal, as their sex not equal seemed;
> For contemplation he and valor formed,
> For softness she and sweet attractive grace,
> He for God only, she for God in him.   (4.296–9)

This passage has put off many readers (including me, when I first read it in high school and exploded in righteous indignation). The couple seem frozen in the stereotypical and rigid gender roles that were often traced back to the story of creation in Genesis 2 in which Eve is created after Adam from his side, a spare rib.

On the basis of this biblical account, it was argued that women are essentially secondary to men, a superfluous 'second sex'. Temporal sequence was turned into a hierarchy of power. But this argument makes no real sense, as thinkers in seventeenth-century England had begun to notice. The popular seventeenth-century essayist Owen Feltham (1604–68) saw the problem: 'If we argue from the text, that ... the man being put first, was worthier. I answer, "So the evening and the morning was the first day": yet few will think the night the better.'[17] Why should something be *better* just because it comes first sequentially? One could argue with just as much logic that women are better because they come second: God first made Adam and then, realizing he had botched the job, got it right and made Eve. Some seventeenth-century women made exactly this point; Esther Sowernam quipped that 'Women were the last worke and therefore

---

[17] 'Of Woman', cited from *The Broadview Anthology of Seventeenth-Century Verse and Prose*, ed. Alan Rudrum, Joseph Black, and Holly Faith Nelson, reprint (Peterborough, Ontario and Orchard Park, NY: Broadview P, 2004), 450. The creation of day and night is described in Genesis 1:5. As Feltham recognized, *before* and *after* are basically terms denoting temporal relations not moral worth. Similarly, *superior* and *inferior* literally describe neutral spatial positions: they do not inherently or necessarily imply being better or worse.

the best, / For what was the end, excelleth the rest'.[18] Sowernam also
used the fact that Adam was created outside of Eden and Eve inside
it to argue for female superiority.

Milton's poem also challenges the sexist logic behind the traditional
interpretations of Genesis 2. It questions familiar hierarchical modes
of categorization and imagines alternative ways of seeing relations.
Adam himself refers to Eve as 'fairest of creation, last and best / Of
all God's works' (9.896–7); he tells the angel Raphael that while he has
been told that Eve is 'inferior, in the mind / And inward faculties'
(8.541–2) she actually seems to him superior: 'one intended first, not
after made / Occasionally' (8.555–6). Though Raphael insists that
Eve is 'Less excellent' (8.566), Adam's experience is that Eve's actions
are 'wisest, virtuousest, discreetest, best' (8.550) and indeed that 'All
higher knowledge in her presence falls / Degraded' (8.551–2). Many
readers have assumed that there is something inherently wrong with
Adam's estimation of Eve. But the qualities he praises her for are ones
she demonstrates throughout the poem.

As Adam's experience of Eve seems to contradict his knowledge
that she is 'inferior', the poetic representation of the couple does not
fit the traditional Christian reading of their relation derived from
Genesis. In Book 4, Milton invokes the static roles associated with the
conventional Adam and Eve, but immediately starts to unfix them. As
the couple begin to speak to each other and play with language, they
come alive, transformed from rigid archetypes who represent immutable gender difference into dynamic dramatic characters who complicate our expectations. From the very start, they are represented as
distinct individuals with different personalities and ways of seeing the
world. Each tells the story of their own creation, and in so doing
reveals different aspects of their characters. As with most couples,
each has a slightly different memory of how they met.[19] They have

---

[18] *Ester Hath Hang'd Haman; Or, an Answer to a Lewd Pamphlet, Entitled, the Arraignment of Women* (London: Printed for Nicholas Bourne, 1617) 50 Hlv; quoted from Shannon Miller, *Engendering the Fall: John Milton and Seventeenth-Century Women Writers* (Philadelphia: University of Pennsylvania Press, 2008), 33.

[19] Compare especially Eve's account of her motives for turning away from Adam when she first sees him—he is not as attractive as her own image—with that of Adam, who claims that her consciousness of her own merit makes her demand that he court her (4.478–80 and 8.500–14). While critics are often troubled by this discrepancy, it is refreshingly realistic in terms of human experiences.

different abilities and interests. By allowing Eve to tell the story of her own creation (Book 4.449–91) *before* Adam tells his (Book 8.250–520), moreover, Milton disrupts the conventional sequence which had been used to make women 'the second sex'. In the poem at least, Eve's creation comes first. Her spontaneous outburst in Book 4 means further that she is not only the first *woman*: she is the first *poet*, a proto-Sappho. Her lyric reverses the roles of conventional love poetry in which the male poet celebrates a female object of desire. Eve's association with excess (that gorgeously wild hair that cascades down to her waist) might make her seem closer than Adam to the essence of an Edenic world marked by its luxuriance and lushness.

This does not mean, however, that Milton simply reverses roles to make Eve superior to Adam. The doctrine of progress, which suggests that something made later must be better than things made earlier, was relatively new at this time. It is entertained by Satan who suggests Eden may be superior to Heaven: 'as built / With second thoughts, reforming what was old! / For what god after better worse would build?' (9.100–2). But as a failed revolutionary like Milton may have known, such reversals are too often revolutionary in the sense of circular, reversing top and bottom while leaving the hierarchical power structure intact. As we saw, Milton had begun to question such structures in *Comus*, in which the Lady must be freed by forces from below as well as above, and the action ends with a vision of a very earthly paradise. In *Paradise Lost*, Milton goes farther to unsettle hierarchy as a mode of understanding difference. The differences between Adam and Eve are flexible and, like Milton's verse, not always predictable. In Book 4, Eve sings of and to Adam before they go to bed. The morning after Eve's love poem, Adam shows his creative side, awakening Eve with a love song:

> Awake
> My fairest, my espoused, my latest found,
> Heav'n's last best gift, my ever new delight,
> Awake, the morning shines, and the fresh field
> Calls us; we lose the prime, to mark how spring
> Our tended plants, how blows the citron grove,
> What drops the myrrh, and what the balmy reed,
> How nature paints her colors, how the bee
> Sits on the bloom extracting liquid sweet. (5.17–25)

Adam is in fact a poet too. While his poem picks up on Eve's lyric of the night before, as his verse comes to rest on the word 'sweet', he reminds us also that Eve's poem was itself a response to his earlier claim that work with her is 'sweet' (4.439). Creativity is a dialogue between the two voices. Unlike Satan who insists on his own rigid heroic consistency and individuality, Adam and Eve are growing as they respond to and learn from each other.

As we saw, Milton imagines divine creativity as including both male and female powers: the Holy Spirit is both a maternal brooding dove and a paternal impregnating force. Similarly, in his Eden, the creativity which overflows the boundaries between the divine and the human unites man and woman. Milton makes us think differently about the traditionally gendered hierarchies of order that were derived from Genesis, offering us a new interpretation of the Bible. In Genesis also, Adam and Eve are given dominion over the natural world: 'And God blessed them, and God said unto them, Be fruitful, and multiply, and replenish the earth, and subdue it: and have dominion over the fish of the sea, and over the fowl of the air, and over every living thing that moveth upon the earth' (Genesis 1:28). Too often this delegation of power has been used to authorize an anthropocentric programme of environmental exploitation. The idea that nature is an object to be used for human pleasure or power increased with the scientific advances of the seventeenth century. Milton however was a monist, someone who believes in the oneness of spirit and matter, soul and body. His ideal world also involves a symbiotic relation between humans and nature. When Adam asks God for a partner because he is lonely with only animals for company, God teasingly notes that animals also have language and 'They also know, / And reason not contemptibly' (8.373–4). They may not have everything Adam wants, but they may not be as different from humans as he thinks. Adam's morning song also suggests a kinship between the human and the natural. He points out that as nature is now awake Eve should be as well. The garden he describes is active: the plants 'spring', the grove 'blows', myrrh 'drops', the bee busies itself making honey, and all 'nature paints her colors'. Nature is not a passive creation that God has made for Adam and Eve to work upon: it is itself an active and creative agent that also produces something 'sweet'.

The creative energy of the entire world is shown in Book 5, when Adam and Eve begin their day of work by bursting out into a symphonic hymn of praise to God 'in fit strains pronounced or sung / Unmeditated, such prompt eloquence / Flowed from their lips, in prose or numerous verse' (5.148–50). They ask all nature to join in as Milton expands brilliantly upon the Psalmic tradition in which the earth proclaims the glory of God: 'On Earth join all ye creatures to extol / Him first, him last, him midst, and without end' (5.164–5).[20] They invoke the Sun and Moon and all the stars to 'Vary to our great Maker still new praise' (5.184). The entire cosmos becomes a kind of natural symphony of diverse voices:

> His praise ye winds, that from four quarters blow,
> Breathe soft or loud; and wave your tops, ye pines,
> With every plant, in sign of worship wave.
> Fountains and ye that warble as ye flow
> Melodious murmurs, warbling tune his praise.
> Join voices all ye living souls, ye birds,
> That singing up to heaven gate ascend,
> Bear on your wings and in your notes his praise;
> Ye that in waters glide, and ye that walk
> The earth, and stately tread, or lowly creep.   (5.192–201)

Creativity is not just a property of God nor even of the humans made in his image; for Milton, the stars and planets, the sun, the moon, the elements, the winds, mists, plants, rivers, and all the animals 'that walk / The earth, and stately tread, or lowly creep' (5.200–1) are both God's creations and also active creators in their own right. Poetry flows from the garden as naturally as the rivers that water Eden. Not surprisingly, for Milton the poet the perfect world is one in which everyone— indeed every*thing*—is a natural poet.

Adam and Eve's long and exuberant hymn shows how Milton's Eden is fertile, copious, and vibrantly alive, engaged in 'ceaseless change' (5.183). Though as a monist Milton believes in the oneness of all substance, he loves variety, and wants a world that includes a wide range of forms and beings: stars, elements, plants, and animals of all kind are not only part of creation, but also actively contribute to what

---

[20] See especially Psalms 148 and 19:1–2.

makes Eden. Perfection demands difference, not homogeneity.[21] What
unites and gives coherence to all these various things, however, is the
power of creativity itself that permeates and identifies all things.
In Adam and Eve's morning hymn, cosmic variety and movement is
carefully controlled and organized, as the skilfully woven song keeps
circling back to the 'praise' of God which is the essence and motive of
Edenic creativity. Like Eve's 'sweet', the word 'praise' becomes the
ordering idea and refrain, repeated throughout the song (5.169, 172,
179, 184, 191, 192, 196, 199), and bringing it to a close in line 204
where Adam and Eve praise the world that is 'Made vocal by my song,
and taught his praise'. Praise binds both the hymn and the entire
world together into a circle of being in which, as the angel Raphael
will shortly tell Adam and Eve, everything emanates from and returns
to God: 'O Adam, one Almighty is, from whom / All things proceed,
and up to him return' (5.469–70).

Milton builds here on the traditional idea of the chain of being, in
which the universe is hierarchically ordered with God at the top. In the
ancient and medieval worlds this model was used to justify rigid social
and gender orders, and to maintain the status quo as divinely sanctioned.
If you were born a peasant, that's what God intended you to be for your
entire life. This idea was increasingly questioned in the early modern
period as social mobility increased. Milton's hierarchical universe is
in motion, however. Things are given a place, but not designed to stay in
it: they are 'in their several active spheres assigned, / *Till* body up to spirit
work' (5.477–8; emphasis added). Raphael therefore hints to Adam and
Eve that though angels and humans are now very different:

> time may come when men
> With angels may participate, and find
> No inconvenient diet, nor too light fare:
> And from these corporal nutriments perhaps
> Your bodies may at last turn all to spirit,
> Improved by tract of time, and winged ascend
> Ethereal, as we, or may at choice
> Here or in Heav'nly paradises dwell.   (5.493–500)[22]

---

[21] God seems to enjoy variety; it is telling that when repairing the fall of the bad
angels he does not simply make more angels, but wants to make something new.

[22] Announcing his decision to create a new world and species, God also suggests
something along these lines. He first emphasizes the difference between man and
angels, earth and heaven, noting that he:

The differences between the sexes, between humans and animals, and even between humans and God himself are a source of great delight but also somehow temporary, as all are bound together in a living chain of creativity that radiates down from God and then rises back in praise. The unfallen world made by God's original creation strives to return to him through its own creative powers, animating and transforming hierarchy so that it becomes a vital circle of imaginative energy.

Bad Poets

But from the very start, the story of Satan shows that creativity can go wrong and this dynamic chain be broken. As Milton identifies the good with creativity, he imagines the transformation of good into evil as its corruption. Like his prototype Comus, Satan uses the divine power of language to tempt others to fall. As I noted earlier, the fallen Satan develops a command over language that mesmerizes not only the other devils but the many readers who have long seen the eloquent devil as the quintessential poet. With the Romantics, he became a double for the revolutionary Milton himself, and the prototype for the suffering Romantic poet-hero.

As we have seen, for Milton, however, the Son is the model creator. Appropriately, therefore, in Milton's unusual account, Satan's fall is precipitated when the Father announces the creation of the Son and so presents an alternative model for creativity to that of Satan. Confronting the seraph Abdiel in front of his troops, Satan indignantly insists that the devils were not made by the Son at all, but are 'self-begot,

> will create
> Another world, out of one man a race
> Of men innumerable, *there* to dwell,
> Not *here*. (7.154–7; emphasis added).

But as he continues, this difference seems to be temporary:

> till by degrees of merit raised
> They open to themselves at length the way
> Up hither, under long obedience tried,
> And Earth be chang'd to Heav'n, and Heav'n to Earth,
> One kingdom, joy and union without end. (7.157–61)

What exactly God intends is not clear—and we never know because of the fall—but he implies that in time *there* may become *here*.

self-raised / By our own quick'ning power' (5.860–1)—though when alone, he secretly admits that he was created by God who deserved his gratitude (see 4.42–57). Refusing to join in the circle of praise, Satan forges a fantasy of artistic and personal autonomy, a dream of total self-sufficiency and absolute originality. While Adam and Eve enjoy being parts of and partners in their world, Satan sets himself apart, and so creates for himself a new part to play.

As part of his filling in the gaps in Genesis, Milton makes up the story of the creation of Sin to help us understand how a good angel could have become evil. Unhappy even in heaven, Satan begins to consider a 'bold conspiracy against Heav'n's King' (2.751), and suddenly Sin leaps out of his head in the shape of 'a goddess armed' (2.757). Milton here combines two classical myths of creation. The most obvious is that of Athena/Minerva, goddess of wisdom but also war, who was born out of Zeus'/Jove's head. The myth offers a dream of an autonomous male creation that circumvents the need for a female partner or even external materials. It connects creativity and knowledge, but also ominously links them to violence. The second myth is Ovid's powerful and influential fantasy of the artist's godlike ability to make fantasies that become real: the story of Pygmalion, the artist who makes a statue so beautiful and lifelike that he falls in love with it and it comes to life. In this myth, as in the Son's creation of the world and Eden itself, the erotic and the creative meet. Like Pygmalion, Satan falls in love with his own creation, though less because of her beauty than because she is his 'perfect image' (2.764). Both myths suggest something solipsistic, even narcissistic, about Satan's imagination: Sin is produced by Satan's dream of total artistic control and absolute originality, and she allows him to perpetuate this dream by loving only himself.

The creation of Sin recalls not only classical myth, however. In replicating himself in Sin, Satan is copying the God who makes man as well the Son, the 'divine similitude' (3.384), in his own image. The impulse to imitate God is not in itself a bad thing; it is what Adam and Eve, as well as Milton, do. And at first Sin is beautiful. But from the start there is something a bit different about her. Unlike God's vital creatures, she is surprisingly passive: she pops out of Satan without effort or will on her part, and, in stark contrast to the newly created Eve who first rejects Adam's love, she has sex with her creator simply because he desires her.[23]

Sin only becomes really 'sinister', however, after the war in heaven. Sent down to hell with her father and his followers, she gives birth to the monster Death, her brother and son, and is transformed into the half-female half-snake monster Satan meets in Book 2. For Death, she is clearly an object to be preyed upon sexually, as he rapes her. The product of this violent intercourse is the pack of hellhounds around her belly who, she explains, now literally feed upon her:

> with ceaseless cry
> Surround me, as thou saw'st, hourly conceived
> And hourly born, with sorrow infinite
> To me, for when they list into the womb
> That bred them they return, and howl and gnaw
> My bowels, their repast.   (2.795–800)

As the mother of Death and the hellhounds, Sin is now becoming a figure of grotesque and self-consuming creativity. Her treatment by both her creator and her own creatures shows the misogyny of the devils who objectify and try to dominate the female body out of fear of its creating power. They imagine wombs as spaces that consume rather than produce (they clearly need a basic anatomy lesson).[24] Sin shows, ironically, that in hell it is the womb that is itself consumed.

---

[23] Although, like Eve, Sin tells her own story, Sin says nothing about her feelings, reporting only how others, and especially Satan, responded to her sudden appearance:

> familiar grown,
> I pleased, and with attractive graces won
> The most averse, thee chiefly, who full oft
> Thyself in me thy perfect image viewing
> Becam'st enamored, and such joy thou took'st
> With me in secret, that my womb conceived
> A growing burden.   (2.761–7)

Her self-representation is strikingly different from that of Eve, which focuses on her feelings and perspective. Moreover, where Sin seems to give herself automatically to Satan, from whose body she came, Eve is initially not very impressed with Adam and turns from him, and has to be persuaded into a union with him.

[24] See for example Belial's speech in Book 2, in which he fears being 'swallowed up and lost / In the wide womb of uncreated Night' (2.149–50).

The devils make a source of natural and female creativity a place of self-destruction.

From Satan's fantasy dream girl—his version of Pygmalion's statue—Sin is turned into a nightmare emblem of God's creativity gone wrong: she is a creator who is preyed on and torn apart by her own creations. A key moment in this transformation occurs when she decides to let Satan out of hell. God's decision to make her the custodian of the gates of hell seems baffling in many ways. But it forces her to make an active choice and to decide which side she stands on. She insists, however, that she had no choice but help Satan:

> Thou art my father, thou my author, thou
> My being gav'st me; whom should I obey
> But thee, whom follow?   (2.864–6)

For Milton, Sin seems to begin with the denial of agency and free will. After the fall of Adam and Eve, however, she becomes an agent of destruction, taking the initiative to build the bridge that joins hell to earth. Using chaos as their raw materials, Sin and her son/lover Death parody the Son's making of the world. Where the Son brings forth vital living forms which themselves are generative, Sin and Death impose order by freezing their materials:

> The aggregated soil
> Death with his mace petrific, cold and dry,
> As with a trident smote, and fixed as firm
> As Delos floating once; the rest his look
> Bound with Gorgonian rigor not to move.   (10.293–7)

Sin's deadening imagination hardens and objectifies, building a world of fixed hierarchy. Her own metamorphosis from mysterious sign to allegorical figure allegorizes the transformation of Satan himself from angel of light into the rigid character who insists that he has 'A mind not to be changed by place or time' (1.253).

Where the Son produces an explosion of dynamic variety, Sin and Death aim at static conformity: Satan thanks his children for building a bridge that will create a world of oneness: 'one realm / Hell and this world, one realm, one continent' (10.391–2). Satanic creation is a form of domination and empire building, an endless war upon a hostile nature. The building of Pandemonium in Book 1 is undertaken by a 'numerous brigade' (1.675) of devils who attack the landscape with spades and pickaxes, and 'Opened into the hill a spacious wound / And digged out ribs of gold' (1.689–90). The leader of this platoon is Mammon, avarice incarnate, who, the narrator tells us, will later teach humans to rifle 'the bowels of their mother Earth' (1.687). Milton's language here—wound, ribs, bowels, mother—treats matter as a living, embodied, and feminine being, but the devils only see inert raw materials available for their pleasure. The image of digging out ribs suggests a devilish version of the creation of Eve as the destruction rather than creation of a female body, an act reflective again of Satanic misogyny. As I noted earlier, moreover, Milton seems suspicious of the objectification of nature encouraged by scientific advancement backed by business self-interest (though he was not against all science or commerce by any means). The misogynistic devils anticipate an emerging utilitarian view of the natural world as a resource to be exploited greedily rather than a living organism.[25]

Where Miltonic creativity tries to make us think beyond hierarchies of power, Satanic creativity entrenches them.[26] During the war in heaven he makes the first cannon, suggesting further how the infernal imagination produces violence. Milton draws on an old tradition in which the devil invented gunpowder to show that what the devils make are objects to be used against others. Here too Satanic creation shows disgust towards the body and especially sexuality: Satan tells the devils to penetrate heaven for materials as:

> These in their dark nativity the deep
> Shall yield us pregnant with infernal flame,
> Which into hollow engines long and round
> Thick-rammed, at th' other bore with touch of fire
> Dilated and infuriate shall send forth

[25] Feminist philosophers like Evelyn Fox Keller and Carolyn Merchant have argued for the connection between early modern science and misogyny, suggesting that the objectification of a feminized natural world ('mother earth') encouraged increasing emphasis on the absolute difference between the sexes and the control of male over female; see Fox Keller, *Reflections on Gender and Science* (New Haven: Yale University Press, 1985); and Merchant, *The Death of Nature* (San Francisco: Harper & Row, 1980). The sentence of Eve to subservience after the fall was thus given 'objective' scientific authority.

[26] Milton's representation of Satan as a powerful and destructive rhetorician draws on his earlier attack on Charles I in *Eikonoklastes* (1649). The king is represented as the abuser of language, a deceiver who constantly distorts the truth and unimaginatively steals his prayers from others, in particular, Philip Sidney. Motivated by his own satanically stubborn refusal to change, he stirs up destructive divisions among his peoples, and ultimately is the author of his own destruction.

> From far with thund'ring noise among our foes
> Such implements of mischief as shall dash
> To pieces, and o'erwhelm whatever stands
> Adverse.   (6.482–90)

The language (nativity, pregnant) and images (especially those naughty thick-rammed and dilated explosive engines) are pretty explicit. When the cannons are fired it is again described in bodily terms:

> those deep-throated engines belched, whose roar
> Emboweled with outrageous noise the air,
> And all her entrails tore, disgorging foul
> Their devilish glut.   (6.586–9)

But sly sexual innuendo is replaced here by an excremental vocabulary, as if intercourse were simply the excretion of odious waste. Classical and Renaissance literature often draws a parallel between the erotic and the military: in the battle between the sexes, the lover is always a soldier. But Satan takes this further. Milton is chillingly prescient in noticing how guns can be a substitute for sex, a terrifyingly debased version of carnal knowledge.

For Satan, as for Adam and Eve, bodily and verbal intercourse, carnal and intellectual knowledge, are deeply entwined. He is extremely proud of his own ingenuity in coming up with this new technology which he believes will enable him to win the war—or at least make a spectacular mess. As he brings the cannon out into the field, he and Belial fall into a fit of punning (6.609–27). They slyly mock their enemies' failure to 'well understand' (6.625) what they offer: i.e. stand up well under the onslaught, but also understand well Satan's 'ambiguous words' (6.568). Milton's devil thus seems also the father of the pun, often dismissed as the lowest form of wit. Yet as we saw, in his first speech to Eve, Adam puns rather impressively on the different meanings of *sole/ soul* and *part* to describe their love. While we don't think of Milton as a typical punster—although punning is an essential quality of the art of another great English author, Shakespeare—he believes that punning is a natural and imaginative part of wordplay.[27] For the unfallen Adam and Eve, such language is

----

[27] Milton's early works certainly suggest he relished a well-placed pun; see the two comic epitaphs 'On The University Carrier' (i.e. porter) who is carried off by death, as well as the delightfully adolescent puns on *wind* in *Prolusion Six*. Dr. Johnson complained

a form of intercourse, a means by which they know each other and their world. Wordplay is a way of creating intimacy and connection. Satan, however, sees knowledge as a form of power over others, and uses puns to set up hierarchies that assert his superiority by dividing speaker and audience as winner and loser. Where wordplay brings things together in Eden, for Satan it is a weapon of destructive division.[28]

Knowledge Forbidden?

Milton challenges many of the assumptions his contemporary readers, as well as readers today, might have about the fall. Of course, he cannot change the ending of *Paradise Lost*: his freedom as an author is itself limited by the traditional outcome. Instead, as I noted earlier, he spins out six biblical verses into over 1,200 lines. In Genesis everything happens in a vacuum: Adam and Eve are perfectly good and then suddenly they do something very bad. Milton gives the fall a setting and context, making it part of a larger narrative about Adam and Eve's life and development in the garden in which something went drastically wrong. The chain of events in Book 9 creates a complicated narrative to explain Adam and Eve's fall from images of God into human counterparts of Satan, from idyllic gardeners to miserable exiles.

The Story of Genesis has often been interpreted as assigning the cause of the fall to the human desire for knowledge and so has been used to suppress intellectual exploration. Many modern readers are therefore suspicious of God's prohibition of the tree of knowledge. Milton puts familiar and sensible objections into Satan's mouth in

---

of 'His play on words, in which he delights too often; his equivocations'. It's rather sad that the greatest critic in English literary history was unable to appreciate one of the great joys of wordplay. See *The Lives of the Poets*, ed. Roger Lonsdale (Oxford and New York: Oxford University Press, 2009), 111.

[28] Milton had many opportunities to vent his own Satanic imagination in his earlier polemical political writings, in which he often savagely attacks his enemies, twisting their words out of context to make them look like idiots; the language of works like *Colasterion*, *First Defence of the English People*, and *Defence of Himself* would fit in with some of the most vicious political mud-slinging today. In the latter especially, his obsessive play with his adversary's language is infernally inventive.

Book 4, when the devil denounces God as an evil tyrant who wants to keep Adam and Eve in ignorance:

> One fatal Tree there stands of Knowledge called,
> Forbidden them to taste: knowledge forbidden?
> Suspicious, reasonless. Why should their Lord
> Envy them that? Can it be sin to know,
> Can it be death? And do they only stand
> By ignorance, is that their happy state,
> The proof of their obedience and their faith? (4.514–20)

What kind of God would want to keep his creatures ignorant? But Milton goes out of his way in the poem to show that knowledge itself is not in fact bad. On his way to earth, Satan stops to ask directions of a good angel Uriel. He pretends to be a good angel who is coming down to earth to see for himself what God has newly made. Uriel praises this worthy ambition:

> Fair angel, thy desire which tends to know
> The works of God, thereby to glorify
> The great Work-Master, leads to no excess
> That reaches blame, but rather merits praise
> The more it seems excess, that led thee hither
> From thy empyreal mansion thus alone,
> To witness with thine eyes what some perhaps
> Contented with report hear only in Heav'n. (3.694–701)

Milton was writing at the time when empiricism was emerging as a mode of knowledge. In *Areopagitica* he denounces censorship as unhealthy for a thriving, thinking nation, while throughout his works, he urges us to think for ourselves rather than rely passively on the authority of others. Uriel seems a good empiricist who believes it better to know from one's own experience than through second-hand report. In Eden, both Adam and Eve are deeply interested in their own experiences and their conversations allow them to share their knowledge and learn from each other.

For Uriel, all knowledge is ultimately a way of glorifying God; in other words, it is a form of the *praise* by which everything rises to God. Yet there also seem to be some definite but puzzling limits to what humans can know. Adam and Eve are not allowed to eat from the tree of knowledge, and in Book 8 when Adam asks the angel Raphael about the stars, Raphael steers him away from the topic, saying:

> be lowly wise:
> Think only what concerns thee and thy being;
> Dream not of other worlds, what creatures there
> Live, in what state, condition or degree.   (8.173–6)

Today, when science is seen as important and socially significant and the study of literature dismissed as irrelevant, it may seem gratifying to find scientific questions denounced as useless knowledge. But why the stars in particular should be off limits is not completely obvious nor does it make total sense. God clearly wants Adam and Eve to know of things beyond and even above their own world that they simply cannot know on their own. He sends Raphael down to talk with them over lunch and to give them information that, as Adam notes, 'human knowledge could not reach' (7.75). Raphael tells them of the rebellion of Satan, and the subsequent creation of the world. He uses stories to tell Adam and Eve about many things remote from and high above their own experience, though clearly still relevant to it.

The poem suggests that the unfallen Adam and Eve could have eventually known many things, including evil itself, without eating from the tree. Describing evil through stories, moreover, Raphael hopes that the couple may avoid evil. As *Areopagitica* suggested, through literature and stories we can know evil without becoming it. The conversation with Raphael in the middle books (5–8) makes knowledge a crucial part of the ideal human life. Knowledge is all around them in the garden and can bring them closer to God. It is as natural and nourishing as eating itself, as Raphael suggests, when over lunch he notes that 'knowledge is as food' (7.126). But the hunger for knowing needs to be moderated; like eating, it:

> needs no less
> Her temperance over appetite, to know
> In measure what the mind may well contain,
> Oppresses else with surfeit, and soon turns
> Wisdom to folly, as nourishment to wind.   (7.126–30)

The knowledge Raphael brings to earth is deeply serious and necessary for Adam and Eve's growth. It is also a source of pleasure, and rather than give a dry lecture, Raphael tells gripping tales which include an epic battle over a convivial meal. The fall, however, changes the experience and effects of knowledge, so that it becomes laborious, a sign too of our alienation and narrowing of mind, and, especially, the shrivelling of the imagination which closes humans off from others, God, the natural world, and ourselves.

The mood of the poem changes abruptly after Raphael leaves. At the opening of Book 9 the narrator goes out of his way to tell us that the fall is imminent:

> I now must change
> Those notes to tragic; foul distrust, and breach
> Disloyal on the part of man, revolt,
> And disobedience; on the part of Heav'n,
> Now alienated, distance and distaste,
> Anger and just rebuke, and judgement giv'n,
> That brought into this world a world of woe,
> Sin and her shadow Death, and Misery,
> Death's harbinger.   (9.5–13)

This is a great example of what poetry can do that dogma can't. As I suggested earlier, God's authoritative insistence in Book 3 that his foreknowledge does not determine Adam and Eve's fall just doesn't seem completely convincing. Here, Milton brilliantly uses the technique of foreshadowing to make us see the action from God's point of view: *we* too already know what is going to happen, but our foreknowledge doesn't make it happen.

The narrator's rather melodramatic proclamation of impending disaster also exposes the enormous gap between our knowledge and that of the couple. The poem is split between two perspectives on what is happening. For the narrator and readers, what we are watching is already in the past: it is something that has already happened and which therefore seems inevitable. But for Adam and Eve, it is what is happening in the present, and its outcome is still unknown. Our foresight puts us on guard and makes us watch with suspicion the conversation that occurs between Adam and Eve that morning. Rising as usual, Adam and Eve have a difference of opinion about the best way to accomplish their work. Because we know what is about to happen, the disagreement between the two can easily strike us as unsettling: a sign that the Edenic honeymoon is over. Yet it is not in itself a bad thing. In fact, it seems inevitable given Milton's view of Eden as a world of variety. As genuine individuals, with distinct points of view, Adam and Eve are bound to have differences of opinion. In *Areopagitica*, Milton had argued that disagreement and debate are essential to a healthy society which resists the temptations of easy conformity and superficial agreement.

Nor is the fact that the couple separate inherently wrong, even though it proves fatal. One of the advantages of being partners, rather than still inseparable parts of a single body, is that the couple may at times part and be apart as a way of making their relationship more interesting. From the very start of their relationship when Eve is taken from Adam's body, their mutual pleasure is predicated on division, and in Book 8 Eve leaves the conversation with Raphael and goes off on her own for a while. Milton makes it clear that she does not go because she lacks intelligence or interest in science—she herself first raised the topic of the stars in Book 4.657–8. But with imagination and sensitivity Eve realizes that her absence will in effect extend the conversation, as Adam can later tell her what Raphael said. The couple can keep the conversation going and deepen it, prolonging the pleasure of knowledge by making it more fully a part of their private verbal and sexual intercourse. Not only will Adam 'intermix / Grateful digressions' (8.54–5) with the account, elaborating and finding his own words for what Raphael has said, but he will also add kisses, not to mention some deliciously suggestive 'conjugal caresses' (8.56), to his version. His pedagogical style is clearly quite different from that of Raphael, and appropriate for Milton's humans whose most deeply intellectual knowledge involves the body, and specifically sexuality.

The conversation between Adam and Eve does not therefore necessitate the fall. But it *does* explain why Eve is alone when she meets the serpent. While in Genesis the two falls seem almost simultaneous, Milton draws the action out by giving us two distinct falls which take place at different times and with very different causes. Eve's is the longer and most complicated. Although her actions are disastrous, her motives come from her strengths as well as weaknesses. Approaching her alone in the form of the snake, Satan first tries to woo her through flattery. He assumes that she is the weaker sex, an easier target whom he can trick through female vanity. Eve, however, is not impressed by his 'overpraising' (9.615) of her beauty and power. Still, she is intrigued that a snake can talk. This gives Satan another opening. To explain his unusual abilities, Satan tells her a plausible story, in which the snake ate of the fruit and not only did not die but gained intelligence as well as the power of speech.

The genius of this cunning fiction is that it seems to correspond to much of what Eve has heard about God's plans for humans and Eden generally: that everything is supposed to grow and rise to a higher form through knowledge. Satan thus jumbles the information given to the couple by Raphael, suggesting that Eve can speed up the process of ascent by eating from the tree of knowledge. He presents the fruit as a kind of fast food, a miraculous substance that, as Eve herself speculates, can 'feed at once both body and mind' (9.779). Where Raphael says that "knowledge is *as* food" (7.126; my emphasis), Satan says knowledge *is* food.

Everything that the snake says is reasonable, but it is of course based on a false premise which Eve cannot know: he is not really a snake and he never ate the fruit. In the discussion that morning, Adam had warned Eve of the limits of reason:

> But God left free the will, for what obeys
> Reason, is free, and reason he made right,
> But bid her well beware, and still erect,
> Least by some fair appearing good surprised
> She dictate false, and misinform the will
> To do what God expressly hath forbid.   (9.351–6)

Eve's will follows reason, but reason cannot tell her that the snake is not a real snake—an idea that in the context of Eve's knowledge in fact seems quite unreasonable. While reason is an essential guide to human action, it is, as *Comus* also showed us, limited as a mode of knowledge. It cannot by itself tell good from evil.

Eve carefully thinks through the snake's story, trying to understand the argument and logic. Adam's fall is much more rushed as he does not think enough. Like those of Eve, however, his motives are not in themselves bad. When he finds that Eve is fallen, he immediately announces that he is too:

> And me with thee hath ruined, for with thee
> Certain my resolution is to die;
> How can I live without thee, how forgo
> Thy sweet converse and love so dearly joined,
> To live again in these wild woods forlorn?
> Should God create another Eve, and I

> Another rib afford, yet loss of thee
> Would never from my heart; no no, I feel
> The link of nature draw me: flesh of flesh,
> Bone of my bone thou art, and from thy state
> Mine never shall be parted, bliss or woe.   (9.906–16)

Where Eve approached the fruit through reason, Adam's response is purely emotional. It is completely human and understandable, and we might indeed like him less if he had done anything else. Yet it also seems rather rash and perhaps even unimaginative. Adam does not even consider that there might be other options, but assumes that the jig is up. 'Submitting to what *seemed* remediless' (919; emphasis added), he too eats the fruit. We can now never know if it *was* indeed remediless, or if there might have been another possible course of action. What if, for example, Adam had gone to God and pleaded that Eve made an understandable error? The story that Raphael tells in Books 5-6 of the angel Abdiel who was first deceived by Satan and lured away from heaven but then returned to God, shows that it is possible to make a mistake and repent.[29] But when Adam eats the fruit it closes off the possibility of imagining other endings to the story, hurling us from Milton's glorious imaginary world into our own.

The effect of the fall appears immediately in the verbal and sexual intercourse between Adam and Eve. Satan's solipsistic and aggressive creativity comes to earth. After eating the fruit, Adam is aroused to imaginative and erotic play:

> he on Eve
> Began to cast lascivious eyes, she him
> As wantonly repaid; in lust they burn:
> Till Adam thus gan Eve to dalliance move.
>
>   Eve, now I see thou art exact of taste,
> And elegant, of sapience no small part,
> Since to each meaning savor we apply,
> And palate call judicious.   (9.1013–20)

---

[29] Similarly, in *Areopagitica*, Milton urges Parliament to change its mind about imposing censorship, arguing that we all make mistakes, but 'to redress willingly and speedily what hath been erred,…is a virtue,…whereof none can participate but greatest and wisest men' (Kerrigan, 966). Milton's arguments for divorce insist further that reform and redress must be always open to those who make honest errors.

As we saw, in their earlier dialogues wordplay had been a way of expressing love, wonder, and respect. Punning on *taste, sapience, savor, palate*, Adam condescendingly mocks the fall as a joke they don't need to take seriously. The way the partners look at each other is telling, as is the fact that Eve, while clearly aroused also, does not reply. For the blind Milton as for modern theorists, the gaze can be an instrument of objectification.[30] Even as the couple go off to make love, a distance has opened up between them. As in the war in heaven, puns now push people apart rather than bringing them together. Sex is no longer satisfying, and its aftermath is regret and despair that leaves them both at first 'silent, and . . . / Confounded' (9.1063–4), and then locked in a full blown and endless argument in which language becomes a mode of attack:

> Thus they in mutual accusation spent
> The fruitless hours, but neither self-condemning,
> And of their vain contest appeared no end.   (9.1187–9).

As we have seen, before the fall, Adam and Eve are presented as individuals who have their own independent experiences and points of view. The differences between them, like those between the various life forms the Son creates, are themselves essential to the pleasure of Eden. With the spreading of Satanic conformity, however, differences become threatening, as the fallen Eve suggests already when she urges Adam to eat, too:

> Thou therefore also taste, that equal lot
> May join us, equal joy, as equal love;
> Lest thou not tasting, different degree
> Disjoin us.   (9.881–4)

No longer a source of pleasure, creativity, and knowledge, differences widen into estrangement and alienation. God now seems a very remote and powerful figure whom Adam and Eve are terrified to

---

[30] See especially Laura Mulvey, 'Visual Pleasure and Narrative Cinema', *Visual and Other Pleasures* (London: Palgrave, 1989), 14–26. Milton was acutely sensitive to the power relations of vision. In *Samson Agonistes*, part of the horror of Samson's situation is the fact that he is seen but cannot see in return: he is an object of other's attention, not, until perhaps the final action, a subject.

meet. Nature falls silent and becomes an intractable object on which Adam must now labour strenuously. Work and pleasure are divided, as gardening becomes a difficult act of survival, rather than the delightful work Adam and Eve enjoyed together. Moreover, while before Adam and Eve shared the same work, now their forms of labour are rigidly segregated by the familiar gender roles in which men labour in the field and women in giving birth. As I suggested earlier, although Adam seems to have a higher place in the chain of being radiating from God, the hierarchy is dynamic. It is only with the fall that male 'superiority' becomes legislated as a form of absolute domination in which Eve is told firmly, 'to thy husband's will / Thine shall submit, he over thee shall rule' (10.195–6). The experiences of men and women are now also foreign to each other: when in Book 11 Michael takes Adam up to a high point to see history, Eve is kept down below. Moreover, while we cannot know things outside ourselves, self-knowledge itself becomes self-conflict. Adam and Eve find themselves divided and at war with themselves:

> They sat them down to weep, nor only tears
> Rained at their eyes, but high winds worse within
> Began to rise, high passions, anger, hate,
> Mistrust, suspicion, discord, and shook sore
> Their inward state of mind, calm region once
> And full of peace, now tossed and turbulent:
> For understanding ruled not, and the will
> Heard not her lore, both in subjection now
> To sensual appetite, who from beneath
> Usurping over sov'reign reason claimed
> Superior sway. (9.1121–31)

Internal order and wholeness is torn apart: Sin is no longer an allegorical figure but a state of being. She is now inside them and us, as emotions and fantasies prey upon their sources like hellhounds.

The fall changes everything. It breaks the dynamic cycle of creativity that reaches from God down through all his creatures and back again. Just as Sin and Death fixed rigidly the tumultuous energy of chaos, the different levels of fallen being are arrested in a static hierarchy that restricts freedom of movement and of choice. Milton makes the regularity of planetary movement a consequence of the fall, as the planets are now fixed in set places and patterns they follow without variation.[31] The human imagination is similarly limited and hardened. In Books 11 and 12, the angel Michael gives Adam a vision of history which shows how the consequences of the fall spread beyond Adam and Eve into our own lives. The presumptuous building of the Tower of Babel leads to the breakdown of language in universal mis-communication and conflict. As the construction of the Tower suggests also, human inventions tend to make things worse because 'inventors rare', such as Tubal-Cain, are like Satan: 'Unmindful of their Maker, though his spirit / Taught them, but they his gifts acknowledged none' (11.610–12). As Sidney had complained, the world is full of bad poets abusing creative powers; as Milton rants elsewhere, 'what despicable creatures our common rhymers and playwrights be' (*Of Education*; Kerrigan, 978).

But the consequences are much more serious than a lot of dreary verses. Epics like Virgil's *Aeneid* were often read as a celebration of history as a teleological grand march of civilization from its beginning to a triumphant present.[32] Milton's view of history in Books 11–12 turns historical progress into an endless circle of degeneration in which human creativity becomes too often a source of aggression against and oppression of others. Another consequence of the build-ing of Babel is the creation of monarchy and hierarchical systems of government. Seventeenth-century royalists, and especially those who believed in the divine right of kings, traced the origins of kingship back to Adam's dominion over the animals in order to claim that monarchy was ordained by God. For Milton, however, kings are a product of the fall: when humans become enslaved internally to their own passions they become enslaved externally by others:

[31] See 10.651–706. For us, of course, the regularity of the movement of the planets is reassuring, and essential for all kinds of human knowledge: it gives us established patterns based on which we can predict weather and farming (and according to some, even the future). But Milton hints that before the fall, the planets were free to roam wherever they wanted; in Book 8, Raphael's caginess about the movements of and relation between sun and earth leaves open different possibilities, suggesting a world of planetary as well as human freedom of choice.

[32] Rulers certainly tended to interpret the epics this way and as a ratification of imperialism. Virgil's vision of history, however, simultaneously questions the ethics of empire and of poetry itself, a questioning continued by Ovid and Lucan and many later writers, as well as by Milton, as we will see more in the next chapter.

> God in judgement just
> Subjects him from without to violent lords;
> Who oft as undeservedly enthrall
> His outward freedom: tyranny must be,
> Though to the tyrant thereby no excuse.   (12.92–6)

Human ingenuity seems to lead not to liberty but to intensified political as well as psychological bondage.

Milton's representation of the consequences of the fall raises questions that seem especially urgent again today concerning the complicity of human invention in empire and domination. The imagination has been tainted by the fall so that, as theorists from Plato on feared, poetry can be a vehicle of corruption. Commodified and debased language becomes a weapon we can use against others to gain power for ourselves. It is a means of division, not uniting but alienating us. Given that, how can creativity not be destructive? Perhaps Plato was right.

The Fallen Poet

Milton tackles this problem in part through his self-representation in the narrator. Epic was originally an oral form, sung by a bard whose presence is itself felt in the work. In general, however, the bard is not represented as a distinct individual but as a type of the inspired poet-singer. Over time, authors began to give narrators characters and peculiar points of view. Milton takes this process further, making his narrator himself a distinct and dramatic character. It is impossible to ignore the fact that this character has a lot in common with the real John Milton: he is blind (3.22–50) and persecuted (7.23–8). It might be easy to dismiss this as simply a reflection of Milton's noted egotism, his inability to keep himself out of his writing. But it is more complicated and interesting than that. As I noted earlier, the epic is generally seen as a cultural form that speaks for a nation and even universal timeless truths. Laying ground for Romantics like Wordsworth, Milton personalizes the universal, grounding it in his own experience. But in so doing he also suggests that the fall has cut him off from direct access to the universal, leaving him only his own point of view. Satanic solipsism is itself a consequence of the fall which the narrator must combat in order to create his poem. Milton's incorporation of a distinct and recognizable voice brilliantly brings home the impact of sin on a real individual whose own life replays the story of the fall.

Paradise Lost is thus both a universal myth and the story of the narrator's individual struggle with evil in the world and his attempt to build something out of the ruins of his time. The invocations especially let us see what the fall means for an author who tries to create. In Eden, creation was completely natural and free; for the narrator it is not. He struggles to write against forces both external and internal. He knows that he is subject to the effects of the fall, especially as he is 'fall'n on evil days, / On evil days though fall'n, and evil tongues; / In darkness, and with dangers compassed round, / And solitude' (7.25–8). The repetition of the loaded word 'fallen' is of course sinister, even though the narrator wants to use it in a morally neutral sense to suggest simply his current dreadful circumstances. But the verbal slipperiness suggests the problem of fallen language and its difference from that of Eden. While Adam and Eve played happily with the ability of words like *part* to mean different things at once, the narrator here wants to separate out different senses in order to use 'fall' in a restricted sense. But in this poem it is impossible not to think of its second meaning, and to think that the narrator is 'fallen' morally. The polysemy of words is now a mark of guilt and source of anxiety. In Eden, the multiplicity of meaning was, like the garden's abundance, a source of fun and knowledge; after the fall it can generate confusion and even fear. The power of poetic language to mean many things at once is precisely what often scares readers away from poetry. It opens up a world of exciting but also unsettling uncertainty that many readers today do not want in a global world that already seems too unknowable and out of control. The narrator himself cannot contain his own words which can mean more than he wants them to. His description of himself as 'In darkness, and with dangers compassed round' (7.27) hints at his likeness to Sin who, preyed upon by her own creations, is: 'With terrors and with clamors compassed round' (2.862). Language couples the two, telling us that the poet may similarly be producing something that may destroy him. While the narrator wants to believe that his creativity is a reflection of that of God, his own words tell us and him of his resemblance to the devilish creators, Satan and Sin. Good and evil are indeed difficult to tell apart.

For Dr. Johnson, the very fact that the poet can imagine evil suggests the problem. Johnson worried that 'there are thoughts...which no observation of character can justify, because no good man would willingly permit them to pass, however transiently, through his own mind'.[33] To even *think* of evil is to become evil. The story of the birth of Sin, popping out of Satan's head, suggests that the very thought of evil brings about the fall.

This is of course a terrifying idea, which troubled Johnson himself deeply. But Adam offers a different theory in Book 5. Satan appears to Eve in a dream in which he tricks her into coming to the tree of knowledge and tempts her to eat the forbidden fruit. It is not clear whether in the dream she actually eats it or not—the crucial action itself is not shown. But it is possible that she does so and therefore tempting to read this dream as a form of foreshadowing. It potentially implies that Satan has 'got into her head' so that Eve inevitably must fall: once she imagines evil, she must do it. But, noting that Eve is frightened by the experience, Adam offers a different interpretation of dreams:

> Evil into the mind of god or man
> May come and go, so unapproved, and leave
> No spot or blame behind: Which gives me hope
> That what in sleep thou didst abhor to dream,
> Waking thou never wilt consent to do. (5.117–21)

Not all dreams have to, or indeed should, come true. The gap between fantasy and reality can be a saving grace. Adam suggests that for both Eve and himself the dream might have a redemptive role. You can dream things in order *not* to do them. Similarly for the poet, you can *imagine* evil without *becoming* it. As Milton had argued in *Areopagitica*, through literature we can know evil, but we don't have to be it. Milton understands Satan, but he is not therefore Satan—despite what many readers have thought.

This means too that although language and the imagination have been corrupted by the fall, these are our best, imperfect, means of overcoming its effects. At the end of Book 10 Adam and Eve slowly begin to repair their partnership. Blubbering on the ground and ranting to himself about his misfortune, Adam entrenches himself more deeply in self-pity until Eve reaches out to him. Although he first rejects her violently, her gesture helps him begin to glimpse hope for the future. From mutual recrimination they begin to develop a new,

[33] 'Life of Milton', 102.

more understanding way of talking to each other, one that in turn allows them to pray together to God for forgiveness. Fallen dialogues are very different from the easy conversations in Eden, and prayer is no longer unpremeditated—they have to first decide to pray (10.1086–96) and then go and do it (1098–1104). A gap has opened up between will and action; the spontaneity and freedom of expression in Eden is gone. God still seems very distant (it takes a rather elaborate system for the prayers to get to him), and Adam and Eve are irrevocably *apart* from each other.[34] The last words of the poem, describing the exit from Eden, emphasize 'their *solitary* way' (12.649; emphasis added) through the unknown foreign land they now must enter. Yet they also leave 'hand in hand' (12.648), and the touching taking of hands symbolizes a partial restoration of their partnership. Where Satan asserts creative autonomy, the couple are going out to start building a world together.

For the narrator also, creation in the fallen world requires trying to reach beyond his isolated subjective self. Drawing on biblical, classical, and contemporary works he places himself in an ongoing literary conversation. In Book 7, after complaining about being blind and in 'solitude', he quickly corrects himself: he is actually '*not* alone, while thou [the Muse] / Visit'st my slumbers nightly' (7.28–9; emphasis added). Throughout the poem, he emphasizes his dependence on a force outside of himself that is needed to create the poem, either the Muse or Holy Spirit. In Book 3 it is only with the aid of 'celestial light' (3.51) that he is able to 'see and tell / Of things invisible to mortal sight' (3.54–5). By foregrounding his dependence, the narrator creates a crucial difference between himself and the Satan who dreams of

---

[34] See the description of the ascent of the prayers at the start of Book 11:

> To Heav'n their prayers
> Flew up, nor miss'd the way, by envious winds
> Blown vagabond or frustrate: in they passed
> Dimensionless through Heav'nly doors; then clad
> With incense, where the golden altar fumed,
> By their great Intercessor, came in sight
> Before the Father's throne.　(11.14–20)

The journey of prayers is fraught, as there is now a chance that they might 'Blown vagabond' by 'envious winds'. Once in heaven, moreover, they need to take a new form, and then be presented by the Son to his Father. It seems a very cumbersome and inefficient delivery system really, but one that suggests how much work it now takes to bridge the new distance between heaven and earth.

absolute autonomy and self-determination but who ends up in Book 10 a writhing snake, helpless to control his own shape or identity. The Muse helps the speaker transcend the limits of his own small, fallen self. The poem itself becomes a new form of mediation between individuals, others, and God: an alternative to the bridge of Sin and Death that unites hell and earth.

For Milton, Genesis is not an archaic myth but the story of his own experience and of the world he lives in. It is a tale of shattering bereavement, which is not only a universal truth but also the very personal story of Milton's loss of friends, family, sight, and his early revolutionary hopes. The poem shows different ways of dealing with such losses. Satan's response is bitterness and rage. Passed over for the Son, then cast out of Heaven, he does not hope to be less miserable

> By what I seek, but others to make such
> As I, though thereby worse to me redound:
> For only in destroying I find ease
> To my relentless thoughts.   (9.126–30)

He finds comfort not in creating but destroying, in making the world in his own miserable image. This is, sadly, a very human reaction to grief. But the narrator offers another response, that of Milton himself. In the bleakness of 1660, Milton's life might have seemed to him over and a total failure; everything he had hoped and worked for had been lost, and his life itself was threatened. He could quite understandably have been consumed by grief and hatred for the monarchy he had opposed and which had triumphed once more. Instead of withdrawing into despair and disillusion, he wrote a magnificent poem which affirms the human ability to create even out of the crushing of our dearest hopes. It's an astonishing achievement, and offers an urgent message for us today of the vital and sustaining role of the human imagination, constantly struggling against what seem insurmountable obstacles to remake the world.

3

Milton's Readers

The Last of Milton

Paradise Lost is also of course a classic love story in which a young couple, head over heels in love with each other, are entangled in larger forces they cannot fully understand. They make dreadful mistakes that lead to the destruction of everything they value. The end of the poem shows them beginning to find a way forward together in order to repair the damage they have brought to their world. We last glimpse them leaving Eden for the world they do not know but which we do. They enter our world, where their problems and experiences become our own: their story becomes our story.

While Milton's prelapsarian Eden seems strange and other to us, the fallen world he describes is all too familiar. It is one in which we can feel cut off from others, from the natural world which we too often treat with devilish ingenuity, from any supernatural power whom it seems hard to imagine as in any way benevolent, and even from ourselves and our own thoughts and feelings which, like Sin's offspring, prey upon us. The playful conversation between Adam and Eve has become a battle between the sexes. In such a world it is easy to feel a detached part, not partners of a whole of any kind. In Eden, differences were a source of pleasure, a sign of liberty as God generated things other than himself. In our world, differences are too often the source of fear and, in consequence, oppression, as we try to control forces other than ourselves and cram life into the 'muddy pool of conformity and tradition' that Milton described in *Areopagitica* (Kerrigan, 952).

In such a world, moreover, all human action can seem useless. The vision of history that the angel Michael presents to Adam at the end of *Paradise Lost* suggests bleakly that it is simply a vicious cycle that is stuck mechanically repeating the original sin. Every once in a while, an individual stands up against corruption—Enoch, Noah, Abraham, Moses—as Milton himself tried to do. They momentarily halt the wheel, but sooner or later it starts up again. Even the coming of Christ does not change the world, as after his death his teachings are corrupted by:

> grievous wolves,
> Who all the sacred mysteries of Heav'n
> To their own vile advantages shall turn
> Of lucre and ambition, and the truth
> With superstitions and traditions taint.   (12.508–12)

The angel Michael who escorts the couple out of Eden explains that the world will just go on like this until the second coming:

> so shall the world go on,
> To good malignant, to bad men benign,
> Under her own weight groaning till the day
> Appear of respiration to the just,
> And vengeance to the wicked, at return
> Of him so lately promised to thy aid.   (12.537–42)

The Son created the world, and he alone can recreate it and recover paradise at the second coming. We just have to wait patiently for that to happen.

The image of the final recovery of paradise gives Adam, and the reader, hope. But it still leaves the same problem for the perennially impatient Milton. If only the Son can change the world, what can humans really achieve? Why bother doing anything? Maybe the speaker of 'Lycidas' was right: 'Were it not better done as others use, / To sport with Amaryllis in the shade, / Or with the tangles of Neaera's hair?' (67–9) Above all, what good can poetry do? The restoration of the status quo of the monarchy had made this question more urgent and difficult than ever.

Milton's final years were in fact extremely active. He kept on writing and publishing his works with speed and energy remarkable for a blind man who had taken his time when he was young. He published many of his prose works, and revised both *Paradise Lost* (1674) and the 1645 *Poems* (1673). As well, he completed two major new works of poetry that he published together in 1671 in a book entitled *Paradise Regain'd ... To which is Added Samson Agonistes*. Like Milton's first published collection of poetry, his last is a double volume that shows his continuing interest in generic experimentation. In different ways, both of these last works are about how to live in a fallen world. It seems almost impossible not to read these twin poems as Milton's 'last word': personal retrospectives on his life and the choices he made. Both poems centre on questions of vocation: the first shows the young Jesus searching for the path by which he may start to fulfil his destiny, and the second the means by which the older Samson may end his. If Jesus returns us to the beginning of Milton's career and his uncertainty about what he should do, Samson, the blind, failed revolutionary (with serious marital problems) who wrestles with what he has done, seems to bring us to its conclusion as Milton looks back on what he has achieved.

Linking Samson and Christ was not unusual at this time, as the two were commonly identified through biblical typology, the Christian practice of reading in which Old Testament figures were seen to pre-figure those of the New Testament. According to this system, Samson's deliverance of the Israelites was a 'type' or foreshadowing of Christ's redemption of all mankind. Christianity emphasized both differences as well as similarities between the Old and New Testament versions— generally of course to assert the superiority of the New and of Christianity over Judaism.[1] Most striking in this case are the opposing forms of action: where Samson frees his people through a violent *action* based on his physical strength, Christ frees his through the *passion*, a word related to passivity and whose meaning includes both suffering and love.[2] While the volume assumes a fundamental likeness between these two biblical figures, it also shows the tension and contradiction between the models of heroism they offer. Together the two poems raise key questions about the meaning and value of action. What is heroism? What is a truly meaningful human life in the world we inhabit?

---

[1] For a basic introduction to biblical typology, see Erich Auerbach, 'Figura', *Scenes from the Drama of European Literature* (Minneapolis: University of Minnesota Press, 1984), 11–76. The logic of typology asserts the superiority of Christianity *because* it is a later religion, but it thus also significantly contradicts the very logic that defined Eve as inferior because she is made second.

[2] The root is the Latin passive verb *patior*, to suffer or endure.

Looking Backward: *Paradise Regained*

If *Paradise Regained* seems to recall the situation of the young Milton it also looks back to where *Paradise Lost* left off. It opens as an explicit sequel to Milton's earlier epic:

> I who erewhile the happy garden sung,
> By one man's disobedience lost, now sing
> Recovered Paradise to all mankind,
> By one man's firm obedience fully tried
> Through all temptation, and the tempter foiled
> In all his wiles, defeated and repulsed,
> And Eden raised in the waste wilderness.   (1.1–7)

Paradise Lost had represented the action that 'Brought death into the world, and all our woe' (*Paradise Lost* 1.3); *Paradise Regained* shows the promised counter-action in which 'one greater man / Restore us, and regain the blissful seat' (*Paradise Lost* 1.4–5). Many readers might have expected Milton to return to the scene of the nativity, the subject of his first poem, or to the passion, to dramatize the crucial moment of redemption. The subjects of so much medieval and Renaissance European art as well as poetry, these moments framing the beginning and end of the Son's earthly career had become emblematic of his sacrifice and the salvation it brought. As we saw in Chapter 1, however, Milton shies away from those moments in which Christ appears at his most vulnerable; in *Paradise Lost* 7 he gives him the role of the conquering hero in the war in heaven. But now Milton chooses to represent the regaining of paradise through an episode in the New Testament in which Christ is tempted by Satan in the wilderness (see Matthew 4:1–11; Mark 1.12–13; and Luke 4:1–14). The choice allows Milton to set up a pleasing symmetry between *Paradise Lost* and *Regained*. The first poem tells of a garden turned into a desert, the second of the desert restored as a garden; the first describes the surrender to temptation, the second its resistance. *Paradise Regained* thus fulfils by reversing the action of *Paradise Lost*, bringing history full circle.

The central action picks up on a question that Adam raises near the end of *Paradise Lost*. Told that eventually Christ will defeat Satan and 'bruise / The serpent's head' (12.149–50), Adam, who has heard of the earlier big bang-up war in heaven that climaxes with the Son's appearance in the spectacular 'chariot of paternal deity' (6.750), expects a scene of similar heroism and gleefully asks when it will happen. He has to be taught how to read history properly. The prophecy includes the key to human salvation, but Michael explains that it should not be interpreted literally: 'Dream not of their fight, / As of a duel' (12.386–7). The future battle will be an internal one which the Son will fight 'by fulfilling that which thou didst want, / Obedience to the law of God' (12.396–7). Christ will not defeat evil through a conventional epic combat but by an internalized struggle against the sin that is now within human nature. Representing this inner action, *Paradise Regained* is the alternative epic that follows up *Paradise Lost* by representing 'the better fortitude / Of patience' (*Paradise Lost* 9.31–2). It asks us, as Michael asks Adam, to rethink what counts as truly significant action.

While presented as a sequel to *Paradise Lost*, *Paradise Regained* is strikingly different from its predecessor in many ways. The four-book poem is much shorter than *Paradise Lost*. It is what is called a 'brief epic'—a form that itself seems rather paradoxical given the epic's usual association with length. Abridged in length, Milton's poem also seems cut back in terms of its imagery and language to reflect a desert-like fallen world in which creativity is damaged. It's as if Milton were pruning his own fertile imagination lest it get out of his control: abandoning the rich, luxurious poetics he had used to describe an unfallen world, he confines himself to a spartan landscape and a simple repetitive plot of temptation offered and turned down. There are few similes and fewer references to classical figures. Structurally too the poem is quite stream-lined: though other characters appear briefly, including God, the disciples, and Jesus's mother Mary, the spotlight is on the dialogue between the two central characters, foregrounding starkly the conflict between good and evil.

As in *Paradise Lost*, good and evil are identified as forms and uses of language. The Son denounces Satan early on as the father of falsehood:

> lying is thy sustenance, thy food.
> Yet thou pretend'st to truth; all oracles
> By thee are giv'n, and what confessed more true
> Among the nations? That hath been thy craft,
> By mixing somewhat true to vent more lies.
> But what have been thy answers, what but dark
> Ambiguous and with double sense deluding. (1.429–35)

The contrast between luxurious and pared down language is itself central to the poem, as Milton replays the debate between Comus and the Lady. The essential war between good and evil is a battle between types and uses of poetry. Like Comus, the eloquent Satan is associated with language that hides the truth; like the Lady, the Son uses more restrained speech to reveal the truth. The Son's plain style cuts through the Satanic equivocation:

> So spake Israel's true King, and to the fiend
> Made answer meet, that made void all his wiles.
> So fares it when with truth falsehood contends.   (3.441–3)

As the 'Word' made flesh, the Son redeems not only mankind but poetry itself, purifying it as Milton himself creates a new desert style that reflects the world he, and we, inhabit.

The poem begins shortly after the Son's baptism in which a dove representing the Holy Spirit appears and proclaims him the Son of God. Jesus retreats to the desert to ponder the significance of this. What does it mean to be Son of God? Who is he, and what is he supposed to do with his life? The Son faces a question not all that different from that of the early Milton, or indeed of any earnest young man or woman eager to do something that truly matters in the world.

Satan offers the Son a number of possible career paths. He describes different means through which Jesus might show who he is and help the world: by being a counsellor to kings, a military leader, overthrowing the tyrannical Roman emperor, even becoming a philosopher. The Son rejects all these conventional models for heroism. He admits that when he was a child:

> victorious deeds
> Flamed in my heart, heroic acts, one while
> To rescue Israel from the Roman yoke,
> Then to subdue and quell o'er all the earth
> Brute violence and proud tyrannic power,
> Till truth were freed, and equity restored.   (1.215–20)

When he was young, he wanted to be an old-style action hero. As he grew up, however, he realized that it was 'more humane, more heav'nly, first / By winning words to conquer willing hearts, / And make persuasion do the work of fear' (1.221–3). In Book 3 he vehemently rejects old-style military solutions to the problems of the fallen world as egotistical and destructive:

> They err who count it glorious to subdue
> By conquest far and wide, to overrun
> Large countries, and in field great battles win,
> Great cities by assault: what do these worthies,
> But rob and spoil, burn, slaughter, and enslave
> Peaceable nations, neighboring or remote,
> Made captive, yet deserving freedom more
> Than those their conquerors, who leave behind
> Nothing but ruin wheresoe'er they rove,
> And all the flourishing works of peace destroy.   (3.71–80)

He imagines a completely new and different way of doing something meaningful with his life: not the well-trod path of imperial conquest but that of service and even humiliation.

While the Son presents a new kind of action, the Satan of *Paradise Regained* seems a somewhat shrunken copy of the cunning and inventive Satan we saw in *Paradise Lost*. This unimaginative devil cannot think of any kind of heroism beyond those that he has known before. As far as he can see, the Son is not saving the world, he is simply rejecting it. At the opening of Book 3, Satan therefore nags him that he is wasting his life and God-given gifts:

> These godlike virtues wherefore dost thou hide?
> Affecting private life, or more obscure
> In savage wilderness, wherefore deprive
> All earth her wonder at thy acts, thyself
> The fame and glory.   (3.21–5)

To Satan, it looks like the Son is frittering away his life, doing nothing at all. Time is passing him by and he's not getting any younger: 'Thy years are ripe, and over-ripe' (3.31). Satan notes that at the Son's age other promising young men had done great things: Alexander the Great had already conquered Asia! Satan is impatient with Jesus's seeming passivity, complaining, 'think'st thou to regain / Thy right by sitting still or thus retiring?' (3.163–4). The Son must *do* something: going into the desert seems a form of escapism, in which the Son is hiding from his destiny rather than embracing it.

It is hard not to think back to the young Milton, questioned by friends and perhaps even his supportive father about why he was withdrawing from the world into books rather than going out and doing something useful with his life. What Satan says here too sounds very much like the things many of my students hear when they are scolded for taking time to think seriously about what they want to do with their lives and to understand what is of value to them. Even to loving friends and family, studying literature can seem like a pointless and irresponsible escape from the world and reality. In *Paradise Regained* it is not just Satan who is impatient with the Son's seeming lack of activity. In Book 2 we see the disciples, who believe that now 'the time is come' (2.43) to overcome 'the kings of the earth' and 'free thy people from their yoke' (2.44, 48). Excited at the possibility of revolution, as the young Milton had also been, they struggle to accept that they too must wait: 'But let us wait' (2.49). Like the young Milton, the Son resists such pressures, defending his need to take time to achieve his goal, saying: 'All things are best fulfilled in their due time, / And time there is for all things, Truth hath said' (3.182–3). He keeps on telling Satan: 'My time I told thee (and that time for thee / Were better farthest off) is not yet come' (3.396–7). The Son's heroism comes from having the imagination to resist the pressure to be just another version of the traditional hero.

In *Paradise Lost*, Satan's action brings about the fall of Adam and Eve; in *Paradise Regained*, the Son's refusal to act brings about that of Satan who 'smitten with amazement fell' (4.562). With this second fall of Satan, the circle of history seems closed. Yet the consequences of what the Son does are not clear. In what sense does the final action here actually defeat Satan and restore paradise? At the end of the poem, the angels praise what Jesus has achieved:

> *now* thou hast avenged
> Supplanted Adam, and by vanquishing
> Temptation, hast regained lost Paradise,
> And frustrated the conquest fraudulent:
> He never more henceforth will dare set foot
> In Paradise to tempt; his snares are broke:
> For though that seat of earthly bliss be failed,
> A fairer Paradise is founded *now*
> For Adam and his chosen sons, whom thou
> A savior art come down to reinstall.   (4.606–15; emphasis added)

As the title of the poem had promised, this action has regained paradise '*now*'. But the angels also remind us that this battle is one the Son fought *earlier*, in the war in heaven told in *Paradise Lost* 5–6 when he

also defeated Satan and cast him down to hell: 'him long of old /
Thou didst debel, and down from Heaven cast / With all his army'
(4.604–6). And, they point out, it is a battle he will fight *again*, at the
apocalypse prophesied in the biblical Book of Revelation (4.618–32).
The battle has already been fought and won, but it has to be fought
again; the world has been saved and *now* Jesus must start saving it as
the angels send him back: '*Now* enter, and begin to save mankind'
(4.635; emphasis added). What has happened? What has the Son
done, and what does it really *mean*?

And Further Backward: *Samson Agonistes*

Milton's brief epic thus seems to repeat and reverse the action of its
prequel, by showing the regaining of what was lost to bring history full
circle. Yet like *Paradise Lost*, *Paradise Regained* ends with a beginning, as
the Son leaves the desert to start regaining paradise all over again. For
readers of 1671 especially, moreover, the poem was not the end of the
volume, but instead the first of a double bill. The decision to print
Samson Agonistes following *Paradise Regained* in the volume was quite provocative. We don't know whose idea it was to pair the poems and
arrange them in this order. At this time, authors, especially blind ones,
did not usually have much control over the publication of their works.
Yet it is hard to think that Milton was not involved in some way, given
his practice of pairing works as well as his care in writing.

The title of the volume *Paradise Regain'd . . . To which is Added Samson
Agonistes* puts the emphasis on the first poem, so that readers might
think that *Samson* was just thrown in at the end, something superfluous, added perhaps to pad the volume for better sales. As I have suggested, however, the two stories are traditionally connected through
typology, and seem relevant to key moments in Milton's own life.
There is a logical progression at one level, as we turn from a story of
a young man at the start of his life to an older one at the end of his.
Yet the sequencing of works reverses biblical chronology and seems in
many ways regressive. If Milton had put *Samson* first in the volume,
the two poems would have presented a neat piece of typology: we
would read the story of the Old Testament hero first and then move
on to the new, improved, New Testament fulfilment. Samson would
be the historically earlier and morally inferior version of Christ, an

old-style epic hero from whom Christ distinguishes himself when he manifests a new form of heroism. Instead, the reading experience takes us *backwards* in time, thwarting any expectation of historical progression. We move from a new kind of heroic action back to exactly the kind of traditional heroism that the Son denounced as brutal, from a hero who stands and will not fall to one who has already fallen before the poem even starts. As modern readers especially, we might expect to move towards a conclusion which answers our questions and reveals the meaning of the volume as a whole, and perhaps even of Milton's life. But the sequence stumps us and denies us a sense of triumphant progress towards understanding. Expecting to go forwards, we seem to be always going backwards: as Milton suggested in *Paradise Lost* 11–12, we are stuck making the same mistakes over and over, never getting anywhere.

Even poetically, the collection seems to circle back to an earlier period in Milton's writing: *Samson* freely uses rhyme, complex imagery, and sometimes rather striking mixed metaphors.[3] The huge Old Testament warrior known for his uncontrollable sexual appetite seems to require a poetics more excessive than the language of restraint that suits the temperate Son. Blind and bound in chains, however, Samson is no longer the kind of action hero he used to be and can fight with others only verbally. As in *Paradise Regained*, the main action of *Samson Agonistes* revolves around debate, as the seemingly helpless Samson talks with some friends—a Chorus of Israelites and his kindly father, Manoa—as well as some foes—his treacherous wife Dalila, and the Philistine warrior Harapha—who come to see him in his state of humiliation. However, through these arguments with others Samson regains hope and his physical strength and, in one last spectacular feat of heroism, pulls down the theatre of the Philistines killing many of their nobles, as well as himself. While *Paradise Regained* ends with a beginning, as the Son starts out on his new career, *Samson* comes to a definitive, and bloody, conclusion with the end of Samson's career and life. Bringing the entire volume to a violent end, Samson's story of temptation, fall, and recovery of powers seems potentially a version of *Paradise Lost* and *Regained* put together.

---

[3] Some critics have therefore argued that the poem was written at an earlier stage in Milton's career.

But the poem does not actually close with Samson's death, which, as in Greek tragedy, takes place off stage and is only reported through a messenger. His account is then followed by a long exchange between the Chorus and Manoa as they grapple with understanding what has happened. Hearing of Samson's death, his well-intentioned father is at first, understandably, devastated: 'The worst indeed, O all my hope's defeated / To free him hence!' (1571–2). But when he and the Chorus hear that Samson destroyed so many enemies they begin to rejoice. What looked like a tragedy is in fact a cause of celebration; despite his mistakes, this son has justified his loving father's hopes and dreams and made him proud. The Chorus thus sees what has happened as a lesson that we should trust God to make things right in the end no matter how bad things look. The last lines offer last lines offer us this concluding comfort:

> All is best, though we oft doubt,
> What th' unsearchable dispose
> Of highest wisdom brings about,
> And ever best found in the close.
> Oft he seems to hide his face,
> But unexpectedly returns
> And to his faithful champion hath in place
> Bore witness gloriously; whence Gaza mourns
> And all that band them to resist
> His uncontrollable intent;
> His servants he with new acquist
> Of true experience from this great event
> With peace and consolation hath dismissed,
> And calm of mind, all passion spent.   (1745–58)

Though Samson has died, the surviving Israelites find meaning and hope in his death. Samson's fall has led to his redemption: loss has been answered by recovery as Samson fulfilled the divine purpose for which he was intended. With its use of rhyme to create a sense of pattern and order, the Chorus's final speech gives closure to Samson's life and the volume as a whole, bringing it to a reassuring end.

Going Forward: Milton's Active Afterlife

Samson may therefore seem a fitting end for Milton's career—a statement of his own firm belief that the choices he made in his life were the right ones and that he was proud of what he had accomplished. But we shouldn't forget that, resonant as it may be for Milton's experience, *Samson* is not an autobiography but a drama, and the Chorus are a group of characters with a peculiar point of view. The group is anxious to make sense of what has happened, and convince themselves and us that it is all for the best. Similarly, Milton's Manoa is a well-meaning father (perhaps not unlike John Milton Sr.) who always wants to believe well of his adored son, and whose only real criticism is of Samson's 'unfortunate...nuptial choice' (1743)—his fatal attraction to foreign females. Manoa and the Chorus comfort themselves that God will bring good out of evil in the end, as perhaps Milton had also told himself when he grappled with the disaster of the Restoration. They seek hope in despair, meaning in tragedy, certainty in uncertainty—as we all do.

In Greek tragedy, the Chorus traditionally offers a commentary on events and so serves as a surrogate for the audience and then reader. Its speeches anticipate our own interpretation of the action and even offer us possible and sometimes appealing readings of the story. At the same time, however, the conventional Chorus has a limited and appropriately conventional perspective, often representing the conservative voice of a community trying to calm itself during a crisis that threatens its order. Because the interpretations it offers can ultimately seem inadequate to the profound tragedy that has preceded them, however, the Chorus also encourages audiences and readers to go beyond the performed reading in their own grappling with the meaning of the work. The Chorus's interpretation does not preclude but provokes further interpretations in us.

A reader today may in fact have a very different interpretation from that of the Chorus and Manoa. To us, Samson's violent end hardly seems applaudable. Our values are of course not necessarily those of Milton himself who had supported the Civil War and urged the execution of the king. Many Christians of Milton's time saw Samson as admirable, a type for themselves as well as for Christ. Still, Samson's final act of mass murder is hardly what we think of as Christ-like. Moreover, it is not even especially effective: pulling the pillars down, Samson kills a lot of Philistines and himself, but does not free the Israelites. In fact, in the Bible, his action leads to a period of anarchy which ends when the Israelites decide to elect a king against the advice of the prophet Samuel and the will of God (see 1 Samuel 8–9). For

Royalists of Milton's time, the Israelites' establishment of a monarchy sanctioned kingship as an ancient system. As I noted in the last chapter, however, for Milton, as for other Republicans, the invention of monarchy was itself a catastrophic consequence of the fall. So what has Samson really accomplished? What has *Milton* himself accomplished in this final work?

The 1671 volume seems to leave us with more questions than answers. While the presentation of Samson's final action offstage follows the conventions of Greek tragedy, it is typical of Milton to wring the potential out of a convention. In this case, the end turns our attention from Samson's very finite act, one which is certainly *The End* for Samson himself, to the continuing and never-ending process of interpretation that passes from the poet, through the Chorus to future readers—in other words, us! Although Samson may not offer us a model for our lives, the Chorus might. While our interpretations may be different from theirs, we too are makers of meaning, struggling to understand events around us as well as our own lives. There is a heroism in reading, especially evident to Milton. Though most readers of this book are fortunate enough to be able to take the right to read completely for granted, it had been fought for bloodily in the Protestant Reformation. Because understanding God's word was seen as vital to salvation, Protestants wanted passionately to learn to read so that they could interpret the Bible for themselves. In Milton's time, reading was still a heated religious and political concern. In *Areopagitica*, it is the basis of a democratic society of informed citizen-readers who think for themselves. Reading is the road to the highest human knowledge.

Paradise Lost ends with a reading lesson, when Adam slowly learns how to understand the prophecy of salvation contained in the promise that the serpent's head shall be bruised and in the story of history itself. The end of *Samson* and the 1671 volume shifts our focus from the figures of the heroes themselves to the people who are left behind trying to understand what has happened, including Milton's future readers. If Milton is using the final volume as a retrospective assessment of his achievements, it is also to acknowledge that no individual has the last word on the meaning of his or her own life. We can never know the full consequences or significance of what we do; these depend on those who come after us. The meaning of a poetic work especially is never exhausted or controlled by its creator but is made over time by its readers who approach it in new contexts and with new needs. Milton himself had learned this early on, expressing it in the poem he wrote in 1630 for Shakespeare in which he concludes that the playwright lives on in the readers who keep his works alive: 'Thou in our wonder and astonishment / Hast built thyself a livelong monument' ('On Shakespeare', 7–8). The author's afterlife is in the experience and emotions of his readers.

Though Milton certainly knew that he was a great writer, when he died he had no idea of knowing if he would continue to be read, or what indeed his work would mean to future generations. I hope he would be gratified to know that it is still read by many people all over the world. I think he would be astonished though to find *how* he has been read. He might not be too surprised to find that for French, American, and Russian revolutionaries, as well as for Romantic poets, he has been a prototype and inspiration, though I think he would be dismayed to discover that for many early twentieth-century readers he became the embodiment of a stuffy and stifling orthodoxy.

What this shows, however, is that, for a dead white male, Milton has been astonishingly flexible and open to very different readings and interests. The vast sweep and continuing relevance of his concerns make him a constant resource for thinking, and the sheer beauty and power of his poetry attracts readers and, especially, other writers. The greatest tribute one artist can pay another is to rewrite them and keep their work alive not by unthinking admiration but by active and often contentious reanimation. Far from being 'the great Inhibitor, the Sphinx who strangles even strong imaginations in their cradles' described by Harold Bloom, or the bogeyman silencing women artists of Gilbert and Gubar, Milton has inspired writers from John Dryden to Philip Pullman and on, who feel compelled to remake him in new forms.[4] As we saw, Milton's Eden is a chain of creativity, stretching out from God down through the cosmos into even the fallen narrator himself. Neither the narrator nor Milton himself are the end point of this process, but rather the sources of further creativity in others.

[4] Harold Bloom, *The Anxiety of Influence: A Theory of Poetry* (1973, reprint New York and Oxford: Oxford University Press, 1997), 32; Sandra M. Gilbert and Susan Gubar, 'Milton's Bogey: Patriarchal Poetry and Women Readers', *The Madwoman in the Attic: The Woman Writer and the Nineteenth-Century Literary Imagination* (New Haven: Yale University Press, 1979), 187–212.

It might also seem surprising to some readers, if not to Milton him-self, that women artists have also been drawn to rewrite his poetry—and not simply to correct his representation of Eve. Perhaps the greatest, most astute as well as imaginative, revision of Milton is Mary Shelley's *Frankenstein*, which opens with an epigraph from *Paradise Lost* 10.743–5.[5] A central question in the novel is how to read Milton. The engagement with Milton is figured explicitly in the account of the monster's development, in which he finds and reads a copy of *Paradise Lost*. An understandably uneducated and naïve, though naturally sen-sitive, reader, he takes the poem very seriously as the story of his own life, and struggles as he decides which character he is, Adam or Satan. The monster's rather literal use of Milton as the key to his identity is contrasted, however, with the more creative and flexible approach of the author herself. Shelley also turns to *Paradise Lost* to shape her own concerns, as Milton helps her think through the relation between creator and creature. Like Milton, she is interested in the act of creation and its perils. She describes the events leading up to Frankenstein's making of his monster, which he feels requires him to be cut off from his family and locked alone in his 'workshop of filthy creation'.[6] Victor Frankenstein shows creativity gone wrong: aspiring to be a 'new Prometheus', the conqueror of death and founder of a new species who will worship him as their god, he becomes instead a distorted creator who, like Sin, is destroyed by the 'Creature' that he made.[7] But Shelley's creation of the text offers a positive alternative to Frankenstein's isolated and egotistical creativity. The 1831 revised edition of the text begins with the famous description of the origins of the novel in a playful ghost story writing contest at Byron's chateau on Lake Geneva. Far from

[5] 'Did I request thee, Maker, from my clay / To mould me man? Did I solicit thee / From darkness to promote me?' From Mary Shelley, *Frankenstein: A Norton Critical Edition*, ed. J. Paul Hunter, 2nd ed. (New York and London: W.W. Norton, 2012), 3. Shelley's 1824 novel, *The Last Man*, also opens with an epigraph from *Paradise Lost*, and the influence of Milton runs throughout her works. Nowhere, however, is it as inspiring as in *Frankenstein*.

[6] *Frankenstein*, 34.

[7] Shelley's names for her characters are deceptively simple: *Victor* for the would-be conqueror of mortality, and the *Creature* for his object of scientific experimentation. Like Satan, Victor can only see his creation as an object and not as a subject or creator in his own right, despite the monster's eloquent (and Miltonic) presentation of his point of view when they meet on Mont Blanc (Volume 2, chapters 2–9). The modern tendency to apply the name 'Frankenstein' to the monster as well as the creator, though, betrays the deeper identity between the two characters.

requiring isolation, Shelley's creativity is spurred through community and conversations with others: Byron, her husband, and of course Milton. Victor's destructive making of the monster is countered by Shelley's reanimation of Milton's poetic corpus to create a unique masterpiece which has itself inspired later artists. She brilliantly transforms one great modern myth into a completely new one, in the process hurling the epic forward into the outer space of sci-fi.

It is often said that Milton exhausted the epic so that after *Paradise Lost* no English writer could use this genre. But like all literary genres, the epic is supple and changes over time. It is resilient and has found a new home and shape in many other poetic and artistic forms, especially the novel and film. Milton's poetry similarly is something alive and changing, animated and remade by each new reader. Not all of Milton's readers of course become great writers like Shelley. Yet in a way all deep and strenuous reading participates in the creativity that generated it. It seems so strange to me that Milton has become imagined by some as a monolithic, closed-minded authoritarian, a distant voice of wisdom preaching a lesson that I, a mere mortal female, should deferentially accept and treasure. Milton's readers cannot be passive recipients awed by his great work as he forces us to wrestle, often argue, with him. The process of reading him shakes up my imagination and makes me feel an intimate part of the creative process. It pushes me to think differently, to know the world and myself in new ways. No matter how often I read him he is always full of surprises, his poetry dynamic, wild, and growing like his Eden. Who knows where he will take artists and readers in the future? What will they make of him?

I suspect that even at the end of his life, after the losses and disappointments, Milton believed that if he could move readers with his verse he would fill them with the hunger for liberty and a better world that he had striven for politically. But he also knew that in handing over his works to us he could not determine what we will do with them, as interpretation is an expression of free will. Reading alone will not inherently turn us into people who are more profoundly spiritual or more truly democratic. *How* we read is essential. And so is *what* we read. Reading literature, especially poetry, is not easy, nor is it always reassuring. It does not give us firm answers and comforting closure. Unlike history or science, it does not claim to give us direct access to the way the world really was or is, but approaches truth through fictions, showing, in Wilde's words, 'the truth of masks'.[8] Poetry's ability to mean different, even contradictory, things at the same time had delighted Adam and Eve in Eden. But it can seem scary to many readers, who seek clarity and certainty in a vast, intimidating world that seems so alien and beyond our control. Perhaps poetry can also be a way for us to encounter and thrive in the uncertainty and fear which is an element of all complex and rich human lives. It finds beauty and meaning in mess. Poetry asks us to see the world temporarily freed from the preconceptions and expectations that too often govern our lives and our sense of what is 'realistically' possible. Why not be unrealistic and imagine the impossible?

The story Milton tells in *Paradise Lost* is of loss, desolation, alienation; it is tragic and deeply moving. But it is also inspiring, reminding me of what it means to be human: how the misery and loneliness, the stubborn tendency to self-destruction, constantly bashes up against that equally obstinate need to see and make the world anew. It confronts us boldly, not to offer us answers or simple models of how we should live and be but to ask us how we respond to this our fallen world. Do we imitate Satan in bitterness and destruction, or follow Milton, by making something new, beautiful, and meaningful out of the strange bits and pieces of our lives? What kind of world do we want to live in? One that is comfortably uniform and unchanging, easy to measure and master and sell, or one that can seem terrifyingly unpredictable and yet still be a source of ever-growing knowledge, wonder, and astonishment?

---

[8] Wilde, *Complete Works*, 1060.

Suggestions for Further Reading on Milton

One of the signs of a great writer is a vibrant and exciting critical tradition. There is so much wonderful writing on Milton from the late seventeenth century on, it is hard to know where to begin. I'll only suggest a few of these here, but anyone interested in learning about the history of Milton scholarship should consult John Leonard's magisterial *Faithful Labourers: A Reception History of Paradise Lost, 1667–1970* (Oxford: Oxford University Press, 2013).

There have been some excellent introductory guides to Milton written in the twentieth- and twenty-first centuries, beginning with C. S. Lewis's still influential *A Preface to 'Paradise Lost'* (London: Oxford University Press, 1942). For more recent discussions, see further:

Stephen Dobranski, *The Cambridge Introduction to 'Paradise Lost'* (Cambridge: Cambridge University Press, 2012).

David Hopkins, *Reading 'Paradise Lost'* (Hoboken, NJ: John Wiley & Sons, 2013).

John Leonard, *The Value of Milton* (New York: Cambridge University Press, 2016).

David Loewenstein, *Milton: 'Paradise Lost'* (Cambridge: Cambridge University Press, 1993).

For those seeking a fuller immersion in Milton's life, times, and works there are two fine modern scholarly biographies: Barbara Lewalski's *The Life of John Milton: A Critical Biography* (Oxford: Blackwell Publishers, 2000) and Gordon Campbell and Thomas N. Corns' *John Milton: Life, Work, and Thought* (Oxford: Oxford University Press, 2008). Though only covering the first part of Milton's life (a second volume is anticipated), Nicholas McDowell's *Poet of Revolution: The Making of John Milton* (Princeton & Oxford University Press, 2020) brings to life Milton's early development in the context of the poetical, political, and intellectual trends of his time.

Readers who would like to know more about Milton as a player with words and metres might enjoy Christopher Rick's *Milton's Grand Style* (Oxford: Clarendon Press, 1963), as well as a series of brilliant essays by John Creaser, especially '"Fear of change": Closed Minds and Open Forms in Milton', *Milton Quarterly* 42, no. 3 (2008): pp. 161–82, and his essays in *The Oxford Handbook of Milton; Milton in Context; The Cambridge Companion to Paradise Lost* (cited below).

These excellent collections of accessible essays reflect both Milton's variety and the range of critical concerns and approaches today:

Thomas N. Corns, ed., *A New Companion to Milton*, Oxford: WIley Blackwell, 2016.

Dennis Richard Danielson, ed., *The Cambridge Companion to Milton*, 2nd ed. (Cambridge: Cambridge University Press, 1999).

Louis Schwartz, ed., *The Cambridge Companion to 'Paradise Lost'* (New York: Cambridge University Press, 2014).

Nigel Smith and Nicholas McDowell, ed., *The Oxford Handbook of Milton* (Oxford: Oxford University Press, 2011).

Stephen Dobranski, ed., *Milton in Context* (Cambridge: Cambridge University Press, 2010).

See also the essays in two special issues of the journal *Milton Studies* on *Milton Today*: *Milton Studies* 62.2 (2020) and *Milton Studies* 63.1 (2021).

Index